Knit a Vintage Christmas

Front Side

With MC, CO 11 sts. Starting at bottom edge, follow chart for 150 rows in stockinette st (knitting odd-numbered rows; purling even-numbered rows), working designs in intarsia as indicated and increasing and decreasing at the beginning and end of rounds as needed. When increasing or decreasing 1 st only, kfb or k2tog on knit rows and pfb or p2tog on purl rows. When adding or removing more than 1 st, cast on or bind off the needed number of stitches.

Add letters to the top edge of the front of the stocking, between the arrows, if desired. You can knit the letters in stranded knitting as you make the stocking or embroider them afterward in duplicate stitch.

Back Side

Work Back Side in reverse of Front (purling odd-numbered rows, working right to left; knitting even-numbered rows, working left to right).

Finishing

Block each piece if desired. Place pieces with right sides together and use a yarn needle to whipstitch around the entire edge. Turn stocking right side out.

ALPHABET

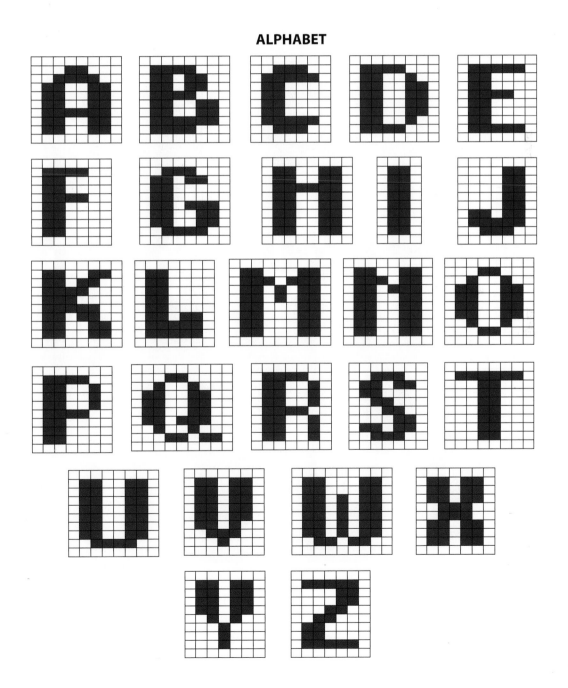

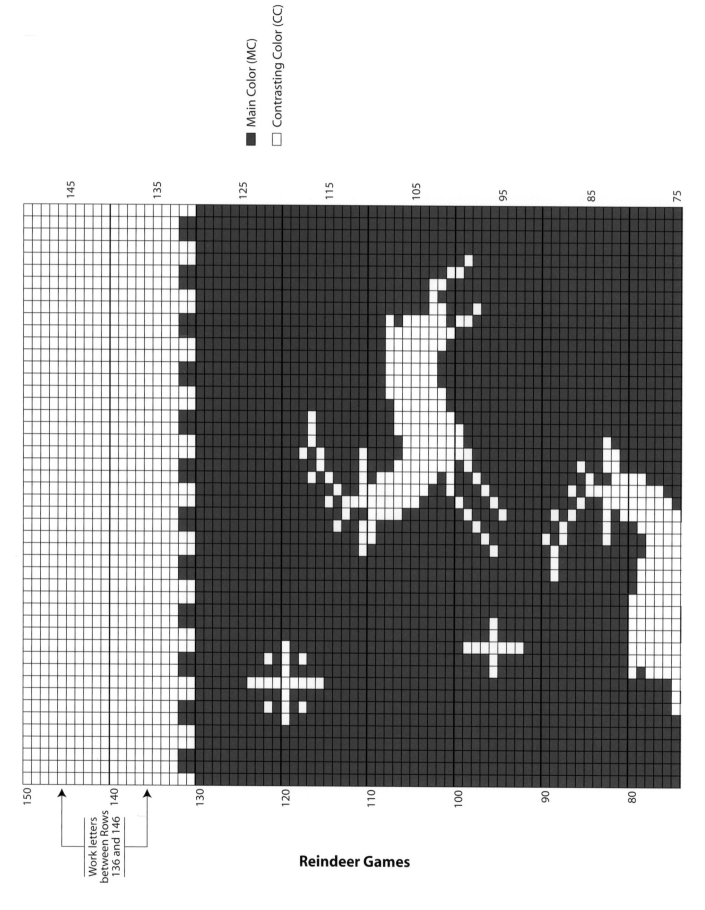

Main Color (MC)

Contrasting Color (CC)

145 135 125 115 105 95 85 75

150 140 130 120 110 100 90 80

Work letters between Rows 136 and 146

Reindeer Games

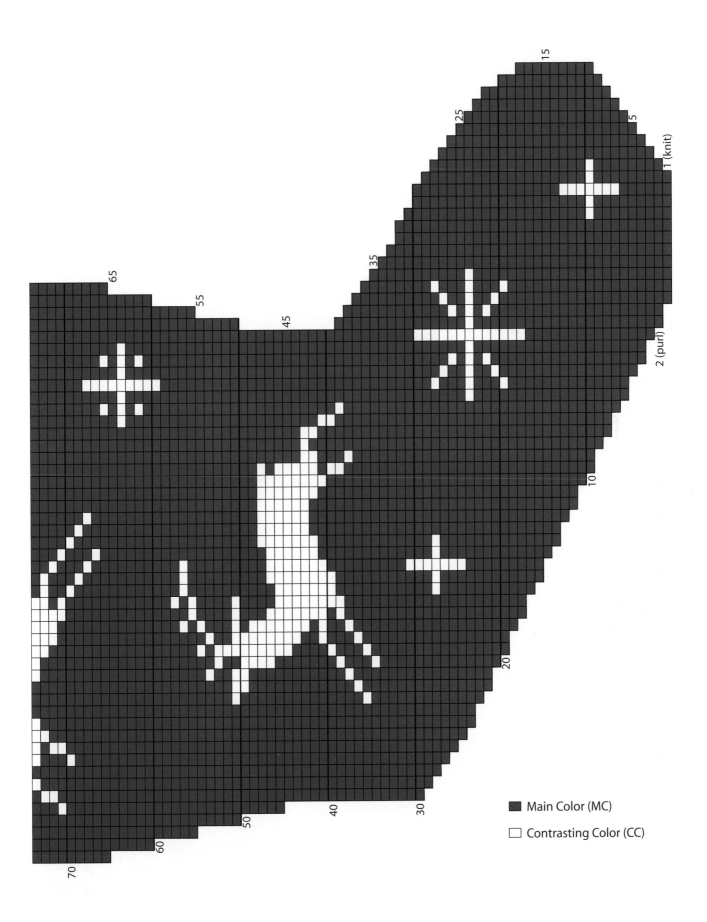

Reindeer Games

Paper Dolls

This is an easy, breezy pattern, with just a little colorwork at the top, and then it is knitted in stockinette in the round just like a sock. Whip up a few of these just in time!

YARN

Knit Picks Brava Sport, fine weight #2 yarn (100% premium acrylic; 273 yd./250 m per 3.5 oz./100 g skein)
- 2 skeins Red (Color A)
- 1 skein White (Color B)

NEEDLES AND OTHER MATERIALS

- US 6 (4 mm) double-pointed needles
- Stitch markers
- Tapestry needle
- Decorative cord or yarn for hanging

MEASUREMENTS

7.5 x 26.5"/19 x 67 cm

GAUGE

24 sts x 28 rnds = 4"/10 cm square
Adjust needle size if necessary to obtain gauge.

SPECIAL TECHNIQUES

Kitchener Stitch

Hold the stitches for the instep on one needle and the stitches for the sole on a second needle. Thread the yarn (about 15"/38 cm) on a tapestry needle. Hold the needle with the yarn attached farthest from you (back needle), and start on the needle nearest you (the front needle), as follows: *Insert the tapestry needle into the first stitch of the front needle as if to knit and slip this stitch off the needle. Insert the tapestry needle into the second stitch of the front needle as if to purl, and pull the yarn through but leave the stitch on the knitting needle. Go to the back needle, being careful to take the yarn under the needle each time. Insert the tapestry needle into the first stitch of the back needle as if to purl, and slip this stitch off the needle. Insert the tapestry needle through the next stitch on the

back needle as if to knit, and pull the yarn through, leaving the stitch on the knitting needle. Repeat from * until all stitches are joined. Do not draw the yarn too tightly; the stitches should have the same tension as the knitted stitches. Fasten the end securely and weave it in.

NOTES

- This stocking is worked top down in the round, using stranded knitting to create the dolls.
- Use felt as shown in the Norwegian Flowers stocking on page 23 to add a name or greeting, if desired.

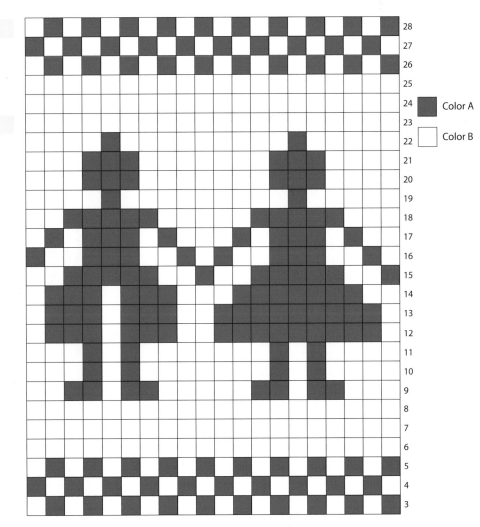

Color Chart

Cuff

With Color B, CO 80 sts; divide among 3 needles (27, 27, and 26 sts on each needle, respectively) and join to work in the round, placing a marker at the beginning of the round if desired.

Rnd 1: Knit.

Rnd 2: Purl.

Rnds 3–28: Knit, following the Color Chart for the cuff.

Drop A and continue in B.

Rnd 29: Knit.

Rnds 30–31: Purl.

Turn work inside out so that the former right side is now the wrong side (cuff will fold over top of stocking).

Rnd 32: P38, p2tog, p38, p2tog—78 sts.

Break off B and continue in A in St st (knit every round) until stocking measures 3"/7.5 cm from end of cuff.

Next rnd: K1, k2tog, k to last 3 sts, k2tog, k1—76 sts.

Continue in St st until stocking measures 12"/30 cm from end of cuff.

Dec rnd: K1, k2tog, k to last 3 sts, k2tog, k1—74 sts.

Next 5 rnds: Knit.

Repeat the last 6 rnds 3 more times—68 sts rem after last repeat.

Continue in St st until stocking measures 15.5"/39 cm from end of cuff.

Heel

Knit first 17 sts; place next 34 sts on a stitch holder or piece of scrap yarn for instep; place rem 17 sts on other end of same dpn as first 17 sts for other side of heel. Join B and break off A.

Row 1: Purl.

Row 2: Knit.

Repeat these 2 rows for 3"/7.5 cm, ending with a purl row.

Turn Heel

Row 1: Sl 1, k18, k2tog, k1, turn.

Row 2: Sl 1, p5, p2tog, p1, turn.

Row 3: Sl 1, k6, k2tog, k1, turn.

Row 4: Sl 1, p7, p2tog, p1, turn.

Row 5: Sl 1, k8, k2tog, k1, turn.

Row 6: Sl 1, p9, p2tog, p1, turn.

Row 7: Sl 1, k10, k2tog, k1, turn.

Row 8: Sl 1, p11, p2tog, p1, turn.

Row 9: Sl 1, k12, k2tog, k1, turn.

Row 10: Sl 1, p13, p2tog, p1, turn.

Row 11: Sl 1, k14, k2tog, k1, turn.

Row 12: Sl 1, p15, p2tog, p1, turn.

Row 13: Sl 1, k16, k2tog, k1, turn.

Row 14: Sl 1, p17, p2tog, p1.

Break off B and join A and knit across these sts. Slip last 10 sts to one double-pointed needle (first needle), then with same needle pick up and knit 15 sts along right side of heel; with second needle knit across 34 sts of instep; with third needle pick up and knit 15 sts along left side of heel, knit rem 10 heel sts.

Foot

Next rnd: Knit.

Dec rnd: *First needle:* K to last 3 sts, k2tog, k1; *second needle:* knit; *third needle:* k1, ssk, knit to end of rnd.

Repeat these 2 rnds 7 more times—68 sts remaining after last repeat (17, 34, 17).

Work even until foot measures 10"/25 cm from center back of heel.

Toe

Break off A and join B.

Knit 1 round even.

Dec rnd: *First needle:* K to last 3 sts, k2tog, k1; *second needle:* k1, ssk, k to last 3 sts, k2tog, k1; *third needle:* k1, ssk, k to end.

Next rnd: Knit.

Repeat last 2 rnds 11 more times—20 sts rem after last repeat (5, 10, 5).

Knit across first needle, then slip sts of first needle to third needle. Cut yarn, leaving a long tail. Holding second and third needles parallel, use tail to graft remaining sts together with Kitchener stitch.

Finishing

Weave in ends and block. Tack down cuff to prevent curling. Attach decorative cord for hanging.

Norwegian Flowers

Simple and pretty, this stocking would look right at home on a mantle in a cozy ski lodge or log cabin. An easy stockinette knit, the only fuss is at the top and then it is smooth sailing. The letters are added in felt.

YARN

Cascade 220 Superwash Sport, light weight #3 yarn (100% superwash merino wool; 136 yd./125 m per 1.75 oz./50 g skein)
- 2 skeins Aran (Color A)
- 1 skein Juniper (Color B)
- 1 skein Golden (Color C)
- 1 skein Ruby (Color D)

NEEDLES AND OTHER MATERIALS

- Set of US 6 (4 mm) double-pointed needles
- Stitch markers
- Red felt (optional)
- Fabric glue (optional)
- Tapestry needle
- Decorative cord or yarn for hanging

MEASUREMENTS

7 x 26.5"/18 x 67 cm

GAUGE

24 sts x 28 rnds = 4"/10 cm square
Adjust needle size if necessary to obtain gauge.

SPECIAL TECHNIQUES

Kitchener Stitch

Hold the stitches for the instep on one needle and the stitches for the sole on a second needle. Thread the yarn (about 15"/38 cm) on a tapestry needle. Hold the needle with the yarn attached farthest from you (back needle), and start on the needle nearest you (the front needle), as follows: *Insert the tapestry needle into the first stitch of the front needle as if to knit and slip this stitch off the needle. Insert the tapestry needle into the second stitch of the front needle as if to purl, and pull the yarn through but leave the stitch on the knitting needle. Go to the back needle, being careful to take the yarn under the needle each time. Insert the tapestry needle into the first stitch of the back needle as if to purl, and slip this stitch off the needle. Insert the tapestry needle through the next stitch on the back needle as if to knit, and pull the yarn through, leaving the stitch on the knitting needle. Repeat from * until all stitches are joined. Do not draw the yarn too tightly; the stitches should have the same tension as the knitted stitches. Fasten the end securely and weave it in.

NOTES

- This stocking is worked top down in the round using stranded knitting to create the cuff pattern.
- Felt is used to create the letters NOEL, and then they are attached with fabric glue.

Cuff

With Color B, CO 80 sts; divide among 3 needles (27, 27, and 26 sts on each needle, respectively) and join to work in the round, placing a marker at the beginning of the round if desired.

Rnd 1: Knit.

Rnds 2–3: Purl.

Rnds 4–5: With Color A, knit.

Rnds 6–32: Knit, following the Color Chart for the cuff.

Rnd 33–34: With Color A, knit.

Drop all colors except A and B and continue in B.

Rnd 35: Knit.

Rnds 36–37: Purl.

Turn work inside out so that the former right side is now the wrong side (cuff will fold over top of stocking).

Rnd 38: P38, p2tog, p38, p2tog—78 sts.

Break off B and continue in A in St st (knit every round) until stocking measures 3"/7.5 cm from end of cuff.

Next rnd: K1, k2tog, k to last 3 sts, k2tog, k1—76 sts.

Continue in St st until stocking measures 12"/30 cm from end of cuff.

Dec rnd: K1, k2tog, k to last 3 sts, k2tog, k1—74 sts.

Next 5 rnds: Knit.

Repeat the last 6 rnds 3 more times—68 sts rem after last repeat.

Continue in St st until stocking measures 15.5"/39 cm from end of cuff.

Heel

Knit first 17 sts; place next 34 sts on a stitch holder or piece of scrap yarn for instep; place rem 17 sts on other end of same dpn as first 17 sts for other side of heel. Join B and break off A.

Row 1: Purl.
Row 2: Knit.

Repeat these 2 rows for 3"/7.5 cm, ending with a purl row.

Turn Heel

Row 1: Sl 1, k18, k2tog, k1, turn.
Row 2: Sl 1, p5, p2tog, p1, turn.
Row 3: Sl 1, k6, k2tog, k1, turn.
Row 4: Sl 1, p7, p2tog, p1, turn.
Row 5: Sl 1, k8, k2tog, k1, turn.
Row 6: Sl 1, p9, p2tog, p1, turn.
Row 7: Sl 1, k10, k2tog, k1, turn.
Row 8: Sl 1, p11, p2tog, p1, turn.
Row 9: Sl 1, k12, k2tog, k1, turn.
Row 10: Sl 1, p13, p2tog, p1, turn.
Row 11: Sl 1, k14, k2tog, k1, turn.
Row 12: Sl 1, p15, p2tog, p1, turn.
Row 13: Sl 1, k16, k2tog, k1, turn.
Row 14: Sl 1, p17, p2tog, p1.

Break off B and join A and knit across these sts. Slip last 10 sts to one double-pointed needle (first needle), then with same needle pick up and knit 15 sts along right side of heel; with second needle knit across 34 sts of instep; with third needle pick up and knit 15 sts along left side of heel, knit rem 10 heel sts.

Foot

Next rnd: Knit.
Dec rnd: *First needle:* K to last 3 sts, k2tog, k1; *second needle:* knit; *third needle:* k1, ssk, knit to end of rnd.

Repeat these 2 rnds 7 more times—68 sts remaining after last repeat (17, 34, 17).

Work even until foot measures 10"/25 cm from center back of heel.

Toe

Break off A and join B.
Knit 1 round even.
Dec rnd: *First needle:* K to last 3 sts, k2tog, k1; *second needle:* k1, ssk, k to last 3 sts, k2tog, k1; *third needle:* k1, ssk, k to end.
Next rnd: Knit.

Repeat last 2 rnds 11 more times—20 sts rem after last repeat (5, 10, 5).

Knit across first needle, then slip sts of first needle to third needle. Cut yarn, leaving a long tail. Holding second and third needles parallel, use tail to graft remaining sts together with Kitchener stitch.

Finishing

Weave in ends and block. Attach decorative cord or yarn for hanging. If desired, cut letters out of red felt and attach with fabric glue to front of stocking.

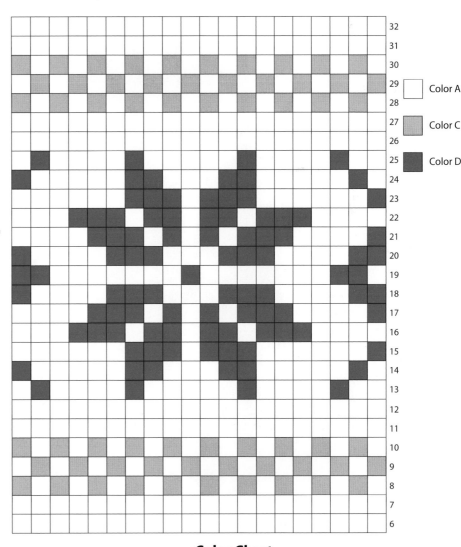

Color Chart

Color A
Color C
Color D

Pretty Plaid

This colorful plaid pattern looks way more complicated than it is! The horizontal stripes are knitted as you go, just like making a striped sock, leaving purled valleys for the vertical stripes. The vertical stipes are added with slip stitch crochet at the end.

YARN

Plymouth Encore DK, light weight #3 yarn (75% acrylic, 25% wool; 150 yd./137 m per 1.7 oz./50 g skein)

- 1 skein Taupe (Color A)
- 2 skeins Burgundy (Color B)
- 1 skein Black (Color C)
- 2 skeins Olive Green (Color D)

NEEDLES AND OTHER MATERIALS

- Set of US 5 (3.75 mm) double-pointed needles
- US E-4 (3.5 mm) crochet hook
- Tapestry needle
- Decorative cord or yarn for hanging

MEASUREMENTS

7 x 27.5"/18 x 70 cm

GAUGE

24 sts x 28 rnds = 4"/10 cm square
Adjust needle size if necessary to obtain gauge.

STITCH GUIDE

Slip Stitch Crochet
Insert hook from front through fabric at desired starting point and draw up a loop. Insert hook in next stitch and draw up a loop. Draw loop through loop on hook to complete slip stitch. Continue making slip stitches, maintaining tension and spacing. To finish, fasten off, insert hook to inside of project and draw cut end through to inside.

SPECIAL TECHNIQUES

Kitchener Stitch
Hold the stitches for the instep on one needle and the stitches for the sole on a second needle. Thread the yarn (about 15"/38 cm) on a tapestry needle. Hold the needle with the yarn attached farthest from you (back needle), and start on the needle nearest you (the front needle), as follows: *Insert the tapestry needle into the first stitch of the front needle as if to knit and slip this stitch off the needle. Insert the tapestry needle into the second stitch of the front needle as if to purl, and pull the yarn through but leave the stitch on the knitting needle. Go to the back needle, being careful to take the yarn under the needle each time. Insert the tapestry needle into the first stitch of the back needle as if to purl, and slip this stitch off the needle. Insert the tapestry needle through the next stitch on the back needle as if to knit, and pull the yarn through, leaving the stitch on the knitting needle. Repeat from * until all stitches are joined. Do not draw the yarn too tightly; the stitches should have the same tension as the knitted stitches. Fasten the end securely and weave it in.

NOTES

- This stocking is worked top down in the round. The vertical stripes are added at the end in slip stitch surface crochet.
- Use the Alphabet on page 6 or 17 and duplicate stitch or cross-stitch to add a name on the cuff, if desired.

Cuff

With Color A, CO 82 sts; divide among 3 needles (27, 27, and 26 sts on each needle, respectively) and join to work in the round, placing a marker at the beginning of the round if desired.

Rnd 1: Knit.
Rnd 2: Purl.
Rnds 3–17: Knit.
Rnds 18–19: Purl.

Turn work inside out so that the former right side is now the wrong side (cuff will fold over top of stocking).

Rnd 20: P39, p2tog, p39, p2tog—80 sts.

Join B and drop A.

Rnd 21: K5, *p1, k9; rep from * to last 5 sts, p1, k4.
Rnds 22–27: With B, rep Rnd 21.
Rnd 28: Join C. With C, rep Rnd 21.
Rnds 29–30: With B, rep Rnd 21.
Rnd 31: With C, rep Rnd 21. Cut C.
Rnds 32–38: With B, rep Rnd 21.

Drop B and pick up D.

Rnds 39–45: With D, rep Rnd 21.
Rnd 46: Join A. With A, rep Rnd 21.
Rnds 47–48: With D, rep Rnd 21.
Rnd 49: With A, rep Rnd 21. Cut A.
Rnds 50–66: With D, rep Rnd 21.

Drop D and pick up B.

Rep Rnds 21–66 until stocking measures 12"/30 cm from end of cuff.

Dec rnd: K1, k2tog, continue in pattern (k in knit sts, p in purl sts) to last 3 sts, k2tog, k1—78 sts.

Next 5 rnds: Work even in established pattern.

Rep these 6 rnds 5 more times—68 sts rem after last repeat.

Continue in pattern and stripe sequence until stocking measures 15.5"/39 cm from end of cuff.

Heel

Knit first 17 sts; place next 34 sts on a stitch holder or piece of scrap yarn for instep; place rem 17 sts on other end of same dpn as first 17 sts for other side of heel. Join A and break off other colors.

Row 1: Purl.
Row 2: Knit.

Repeat these 2 rows for 3"/7.5 cm, ending with a purl row.

Turn Heel

Row 1: Sl 1, k18, k2tog, k1, turn.
Row 2: Sl 1, p5, p2tog, p1, turn.
Row 3: Sl 1, k6, k2tog, k1, turn.
Row 4: Sl 1, p7, p2tog, p1, turn.
Row 5: Sl 1, k8, k2tog, k1, turn.
Row 6: Sl 1, p9, p2tog, p1, turn.
Row 7: Sl 1, k10, k2tog, k1, turn.
Row 8: Sl 1, p11, p2tog, p1, turn.
Row 9: Sl 1, k12, k2tog, k1, turn.
Row 10: Sl 1, p13, p2tog, p1, turn.

Row 11: Sl 1, k14, k2tog, k1, turn.
Row 12: Sl 1, p15, p2tog, p1, turn.
Row 13: Sl 1, k16, k2tog, k1, turn.
Row 14: Sl 1, p17, p2tog, p1.

Break off A and join B and knit across these sts. Slip last 10 sts to one double-pointed needle (first needle), then with same needle pick up and knit 15 sts along right side of heel; with second needle knit across 34 sts of instep; with third needle pick up and knit 15 sts along left side of heel, knit rem 10 heel sts.

Foot

Next rnd: Reestablish purl stripe pattern, as follows: P1, k9, p1, work to last 10 sts in pattern (knitting the knits and purling the purls), p1, k9. There will be 4 extra sts—84 sts total.

Dec rnd: *First needle:* K to last 3 sts, k2tog, k1; *second needle:* knit; *third needle:* k1, ssk, k to end of rnd.

Next rnd: Work even in established pattern.

Rep these 2 rnds 7 more times—68 sts remaining after last repeat (17, 34, 17).

Work even until foot measures 10"/25 cm from center back of heel.

Toe

Break off D and join A.

Knit 1 round even.

Dec rnd: *First needle:* K to last 3 sts, k2tog, k1; *second needle:* k1, ssk, k to last 3 sts, k2tog, k1; *third needle:* k1, ssk, k to end.

Next rnd: Knit.

Rep last 2 rnds 11 more times—20 sts rem after last repeat (5, 10, 5).

Knit across first needle, then slip sts of first needle to third needle. Cut yarn, leaving a long tail. Holding second and third needles parallel, use tail to graft remaining sts together with Kitchener Stitch.

Finishing

Cut several pieces of A and C a few yards long. Use the crochet hook to work rows of slip stitch along the surface of the stocking in the columns of purl stitches, alternating the colors around the stocking.

If desired, use the Alphabet on page 6 or 17 to add a name or greeting in duplicate stitch or cross-stitch.

Weave in all ends. Steam block.

Jolly Old St. Nick

This stocking is extra fun with bright colors and fuzzy white yarn for Santa's beard and hair, but you could also choose more traditional colors and use white yarn that matches what you used on the rest of the stocking. Make the three-dimensional tassel or try a pom-pom on the end of St. Nick's cap.

YARN

Knit Picks Brava Sport, fine weight #2 yarn (100% premium acrylic; 273 yd./250 m per 3.5 oz./100 g skein)
- 3 skeins Celestial (Color A)
- 1 skein Caution (Color B)
- 1 skein Cornflower (Color C)
- 1 skein Red (Color D)
- 1 skein White (Color E)
- 1 skein Blush (Color F)

Optional Color E: Soft furry/fluffy white yarn for Santa's hair and beard (as shown)

NEEDLES AND OTHER MATERIALS

- US 5 (3.75 mm) straight needles
- Tapestry needle
- Optional: decorative cord or yarn for hanging (as shown, or work I-cord bind-off into loop as described in pattern)
- Optional: bobbins for working intarsia

MEASUREMENTS

8 x 22.5"/20 x 57 cm

GAUGE

22 sts x 28 rows = 4"/10 cm square
Adjust needle size if necessary to obtain gauge.

SPECIAL TECHNIQUES

Cable Cast-On

Make a slip knot and place it on the left-hand needle. Knit a stitch but do not pull it off the left-hand needle; instead transfer the new stitch from right to left needle, leaving two stitches on the left-hand needle. *Now insert the needle between the two stitches, wrap the yarn around the needle as if to knit, and pull the yarn through. Transfer the newly created stitch onto the left-hand needle. Repeat from * until you have the number of stitches needed.

French Knot

Bring the threaded needle up through the fabric to the front. Wrap the yarn around the needle three or four times, maintaining a tight tension as you wrap it, then push the needle down through the fabric just next to where it came out. Pull the needle through the knot to the back of the fabric.

Attached I-Cord Bind-Off

Cable cast-on 3 sts; pick up and knit 1 st from edge of stocking. *Without turning, move needle to left hand and slide stitches back to tip of needle. Pulling yarn firmly behind stitches on left needle, k3, ssk, pick up and knit next stitch from edge of stocking; rep from * around top of stocking. Bind off remaining 4 stitches.

NOTES

- This stocking is knitted in two pieces and sewn together. Each side is worked back and forth in rows, following the chart, working in reverse on Back Side.
- The motifs are worked in intarsia.
- Use the Alphabet on page 17 to add a name or other words to the top of this stocking, either with stranded knitting as you go or in duplicate stitch.

Front Side

With Color A, CO 11 sts. Starting at bottom edge, follow chart for 150 rows in stockinette st (knitting odd-numbered rows; purling even-numbered rows), working designs in intarsia as indicated and increasing and decreasing at the beginning and end of rounds as needed. When increasing or decreasing 1 st only, kfb or k2tog on knit rows and pfb or p2tog on purl rows. When adding or removing more than 1 st, cast on or bind off the needed number of stitches. Bind off.

Add letters to the cuff of the front of the stocking in duplicate stitch or stranded knitting, between the arrows, if desired.

Santa's Face

Arranging features as shown in photos, add eyebrows with Color E, eyes with Color A, and mouth with Color D. Cut a few strands of Color E yarn 3"/7.5 cm long for mustache; tack centers under nose. Wind Color E yarn about 10 times around 5"/13 cm piece of cardboard; with another small strand tie at one end. Cut at opposite end; tie a small strand around all strands .25"/.5 cm from tied end. Tack tassel to tip of cap.

Bell and Holly

Make a French knot with Color B for bell ringer and three French knots with Color D for holly berries.

Back Side

With Color A, work Back Side in reverse of front beginning with a purl row (worked right to left) and following chart but omitting colorwork pattern. Bind off.

Finishing

Use mattress stitch or preferred seaming method to sew front and back sides together, then continue with attached I-cord bind-off in Color B as follows: With DPN, attach Color B, cable cast-on 3 sts; pick up and knit 1 st from edge of stocking. *Without turning, move needle to left hand and slide stitches back to tip of needle. Pulling yarn firmly behind stitches on left needle, k3, ssk, pick up and knit next stitch from edge of stocking; rep from * around top of stocking. When edge of stocking stitches are knit up, continue in I-cord for 2"/5 cm for hanging loop, if desired (or bind off and secure to beginning of I-cord, if you choose another hanging method). Bind off remaining 4 sts and secure to beginning of I-cord to create hanging loop.

Weave in any remaining ends and block.

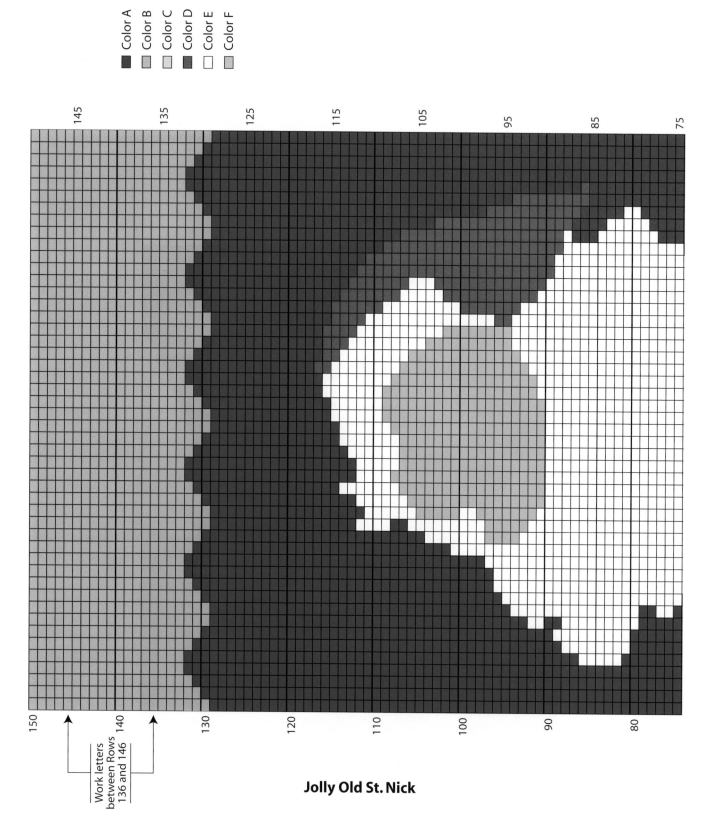

Jolly Old St. Nick

Work letters between Rows 136 and 146

Color A
Color B
Color C
Color D
Color E
Color F

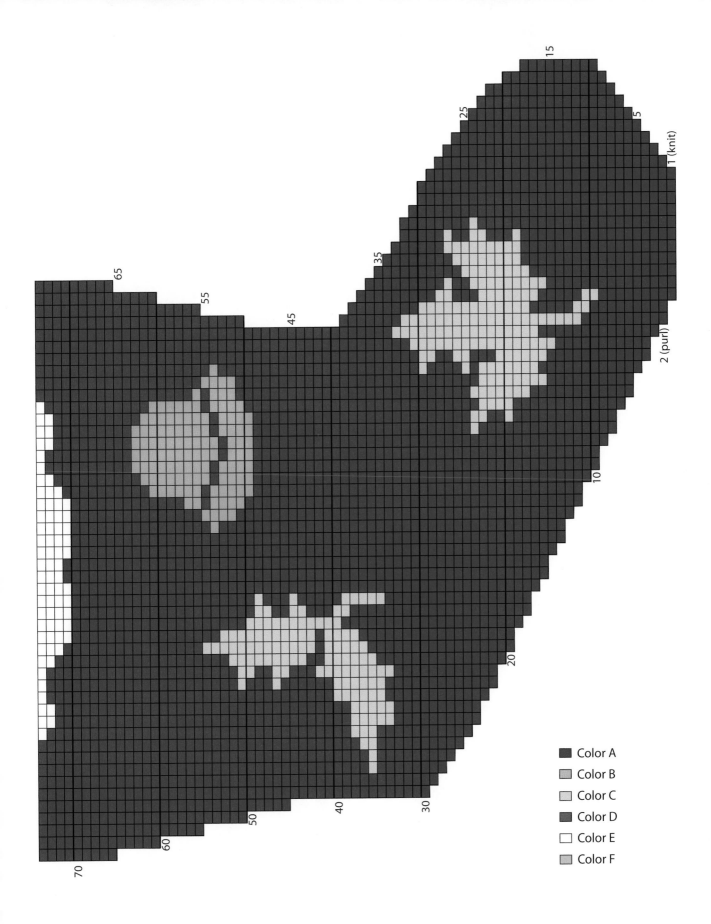

Jolly Old St. Nick

Night Sleigh

This is the vision all the kids dream of! Santa in his sleigh, flying through the moonlit sky on Christmas Eve to deliver presents to the houses full of sleeping children below.

YARN

Knit Picks Palette, super fine weight #1 yarn (100% Peruvian Highland wool; 231 yd./211 m per 1.7 oz./50 g ball)
- 2 skeins Navy (Color A)
- 1 skein White (Color B)
- 1 skein Cornmeal (Color C)
- 1 skein Asphalt Heather (Color D)
- 1 skein Autumn Heather (Color E)

NEEDLES AND OTHER MATERIALS

- US 3 (3.25 mm) straight needles
- Waste yarn
- Tapestry needle
- Decorative cord or yarn for hanging
- Optional: bobbins for working intarsia

MEASUREMENTS

6 x 23"/15 x 58 cm

GAUGE

28 sts x 36 rows = 4"/10 cm square
Adjust needle size if necessary to obtain gauge.

NOTES

- This stocking is worked from the top down, back and forth in rows, and then seamed up the back.
- The design is worked in intarsia.
- As shown, the name was worked in duplicate stitch after the stocking was knitted, but you may also use the letter charts on pages 6 or 17 to create your own name or phrase in stranded knitting as you go.

Leg

With Color A, CO 82 sts.
Rows 1–12: Knit.
Row 13 (RS): Knit.
Row 14: Purl.
Rows 15–148: Continue in St st, following the chart for colors and decreasing where indicated by knitting or purling 2 sts together at the end of the row.
Row 149: Knit first 16 sts (outlined), then slip them back onto the left-hand needle and knit them again with a scrap piece of yarn in a different color. Continue across row following chart to end, then slip last 16 sts back onto left-

hand needle and knit them again with another piece of contrasting-color yarn.
Row 150: Purl as normal across all sts, following the color chart.
Rows 151–188: Continue in St st, following the chart for colors and decrease placement.

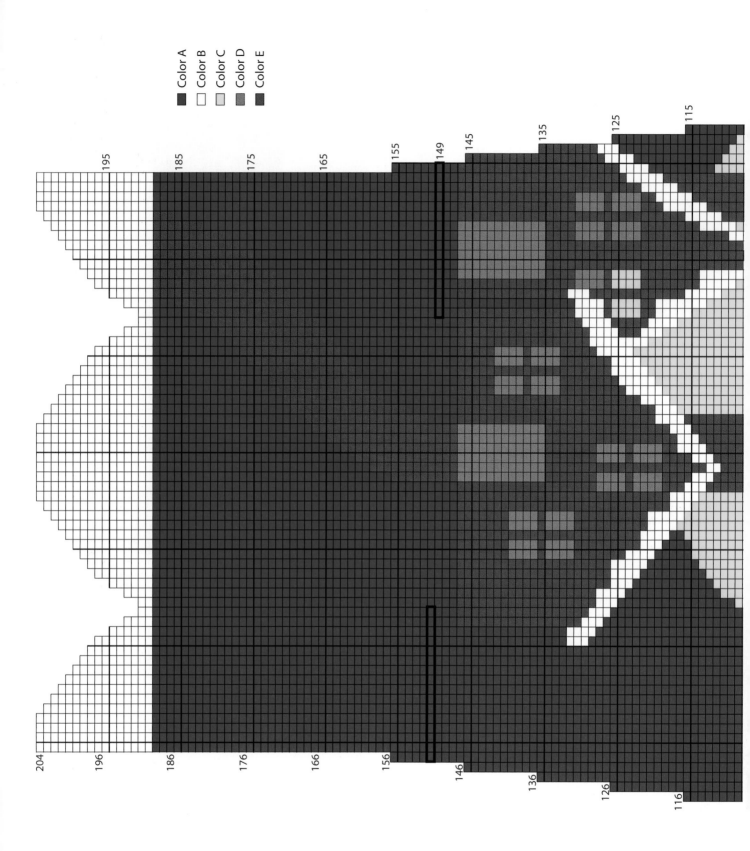

Night Sleigh

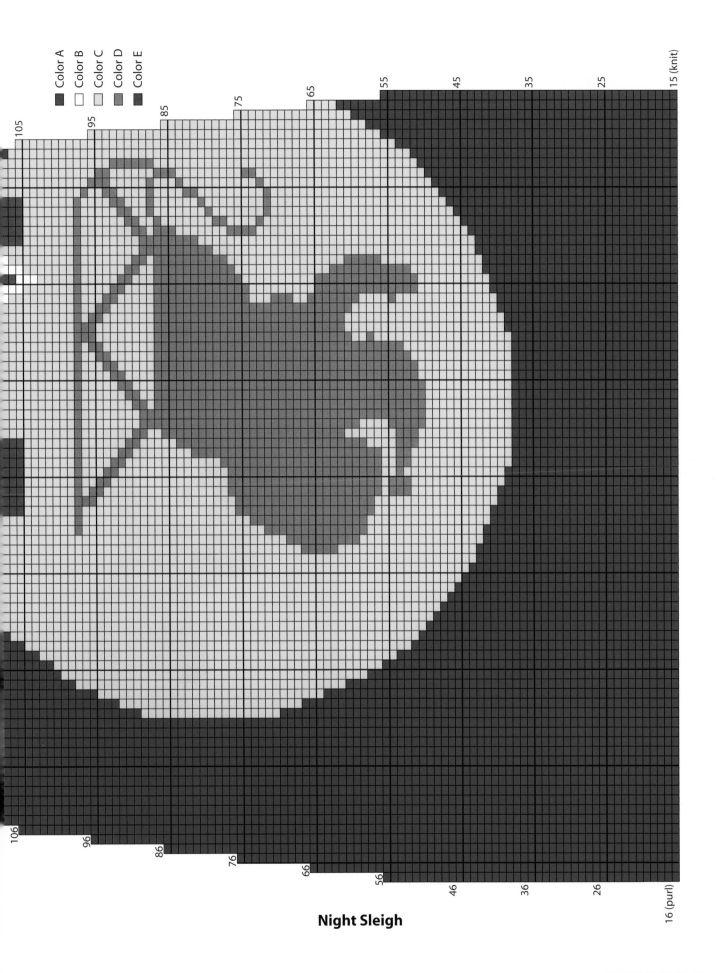

Night Sleigh

Toe

Join Color B and break off any other colors still in use.

Row 189: Knit.

Row 190: P15, pm, p30, pm, p15.

Row 191: Knit to 3 sts before first marker, ssk, k1, sm; k1, k2tog, knit to 3 sts before second marker, ssk, k1, sm; k1, k2tog, knit to end.

Row 192: Purl.

Rows 193–196: Rep Rows 191–192.

Row 197: Rep Row 191.

Row 198: Purl to 3 sts before first marker, p2tog, p1, slip marker; p1, p2tog, purl to 3 sts before second marker, p2tog, p1, slip marker; p1, p2tog, purl to end.

Rows 199–204: Rep Rows 197–198—16 sts rem at end of Row 204.

Bind off.

Heel

Pull out the piece of scrap yarn marking the stitches for one half of the heel. Pick up 16 dropped sts along each edge of opening created, plus 2 sts on inner edge of opening—34 sts on needle.

Join Color B at right edge of sts on wrong side.

Row 1: P17, pm, p17.

Row 2: Knit to 3 sts before marker, ssk, k1, sm, k1, k2tog, knit to end.

Row 3: Purl.

Rows 4–9: Rep Rows 2–3.

Row 10: Knit to 3 sts before marker, ssk, k1, sm, k1, k2tog, knit to end—24 sts.

Row 11: Purl to 3 sts before marker, p2tog, p1, sm, p1, p2tog, purl to end—22 sts.

Repeat Rows 10–11 until 2 sts remain.

Bind off.

Repeat on other side of heel.

Finishing

If desired, add a name in duplicate stitch to the top of the stocking, referencing one of the letter charts on pages 6 or 17. With right sides facing, sew back seam of stocking. Turn right side out. Attach decorative cord for hanging.

With Bells On

Jingling bells let you know when Santa is near, along with his belly laugh and "Merry Christmas!" This stocking celebrates all of these Christmas traditions.

YARN

Knit Picks Palette, super fine weight #1 yarn (100% Peruvian Highland wool; 231 yd./211 m per 1.7 oz./50 g ball)
- 2 skeins Garnet Heather (Color A)
- 1 skein Oyster Heather (Color B)
- 1 skein Golden Heather (Color C)
- 1 skein Caper (Color D)
- Small amounts of Blush (Color E) and Black (Color F)

NEEDLES AND OTHER MATERIALS

- US 1 (2.25) mm straight or circular needles
- Tapestry needle
- Decorative cord or yarn for hanging
- Optional: bobbins for working intarsia

MEASUREMENTS

5.5 x 20"/14 x 51 cm

GAUGE

30 sts x 40 rows = 4"/10 cm square
Adjust needle size if necessary to obtain gauge.

NOTES

- This stocking is worked from the top down, back and forth in rows, and then seamed up the back.
- The design is worked in intarsia.
- If desired, you may use the letter charts on pages 6 or 17 to create your own name or phrase at the top in place of "Merry Christmas," either working the letters using stranded knitting as you go or adding them at the end in duplicate stitch.

Leg

With Color A, CO 82 sts.
Rows 1–12: Knit.
Row 13 (RS): Knit.
Row 14: Purl.
Rows 15–148: Continue in St st, following the chart for colors and decreasing where indicated by knitting or purling 2 sts together at the end of the row.
Row 147: Knit first 16 sts (outlined), then slip them back onto the left-hand needle and knit them again with a scrap piece of yarn in a different color. Continue across row following chart to end, then slip last 16 sts back onto left-

hand needle and knit them again with another piece of contrasting-color yarn.
Row 148: Purl as normal across all sts, following the color chart.
Rows 149–188: Continue in St st, following the chart for colors and decrease placement.

Toe

Join Color B and break off any other colors still in use.

Row 189: Knit.

Row 190: P15, pm, p30, pm, p15.

Row 191: Knit to 3 sts before first marker, ssk, k1, sm; k1, k2tog, knit to 3 sts before second marker, ssk, k1, sm; k1, k2tog, knit to end.

Row 192: Purl.

Rows 193–196: Rep Rows 191–192.

Row 197: Rep Row 191.

Row 198: Purl to 3 sts before first marker, p2tog, p1, slip marker; p1, p2tog, purl to 3 sts before second marker, p2tog, p1, slip marker; p1, p2tog, purl to end.

Rows 199–204: Rep Rows 197–198—16 sts rem at end of Row 204.

Bind off.

Heel

Pull out the piece of scrap yarn marking the stitches for one half of the heel. Pick up 16 dropped sts along each edge of opening created, plus 2 sts on inner edge of opening— 34 sts on needle.

Join Color A at right edge of sts on wrong side.

Row 1: P17, pm, p17.

Row 2: Knit to 3 sts before marker, ssk, k1, sm, k1, k2tog, knit to end.

Row 3: Purl.

Rows 4–9: Rep Rows 2–3.

Row 10: Knit to 3 sts before marker, ssk, k1, sm, k1, k2tog, knit to end—24 sts.

Row 11: Purl to 3 sts before marker, p2tog, p1, sm, p1, p2tog, purl to end—22 sts.

Repeat Rows 10–11 until 2 sts remain.

Bind off.

Repeat on other side of heel.

Finishing

With right sides facing, sew back seam of stocking. Turn right side out. Attach decorative cord or yarn for hanging.

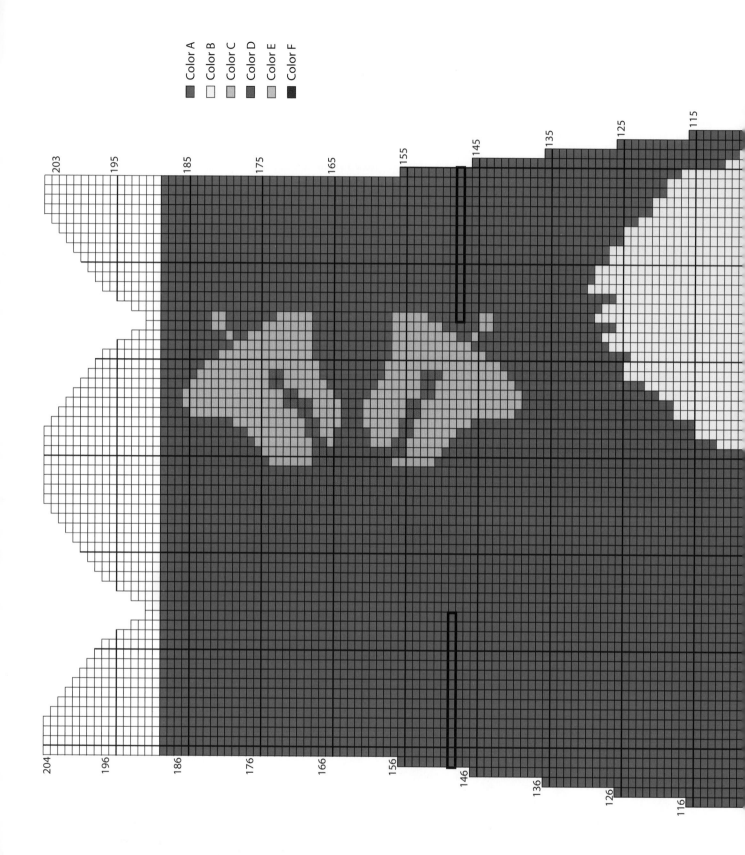

With Bells On

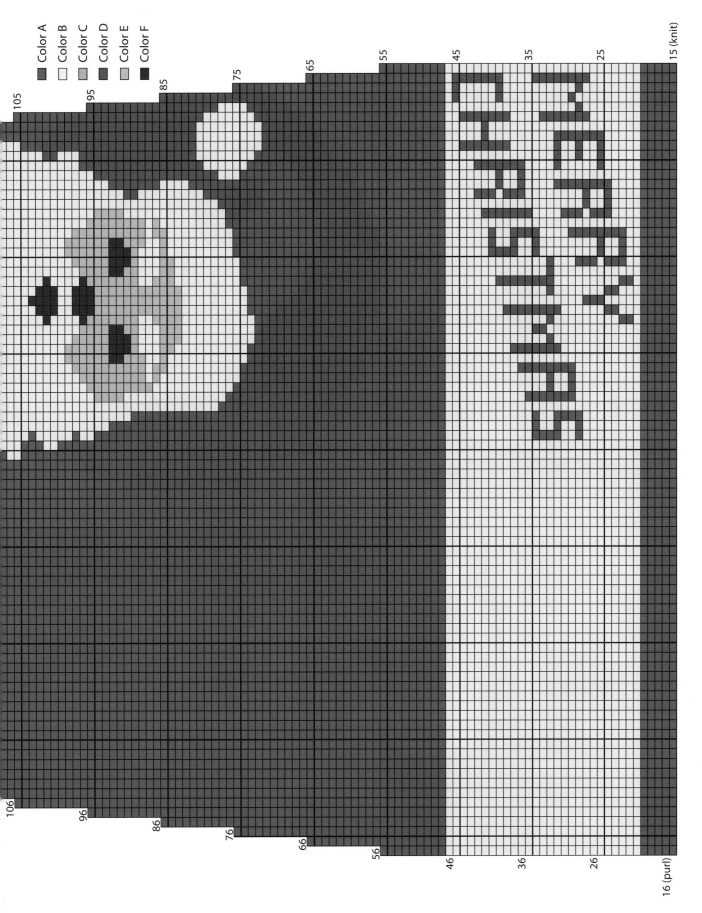

With Bells On

Snowman

This cheery snowman will brighten any room. With black top hat and bold red scarf and mittens, he looks ready to dance a happy winter jig.

YARN

Knit Picks Palette, super fine weight #1 yarn (100% Peruvian Highland wool; 231 yd./211 m per 1.7 oz./50 g ball)
- 2 skeins Navy (Color A)
- 1 skein White (Color B)
- 1 skein Pimento (Color C)
- 1 skein Asphalt Heather (Color D)
- 1 skein Autumn Heather (Color E)
- 1 skein Grass (Color F)

NEEDLES AND OTHER MATERIALS

- US 3 (3.25 mm) straight needles
- Waste yarn
- Tapestry needle
- Decorative cord or yarn for hanging
- Optional: bobbins for working intarsia

MEASUREMENTS

6.25 x 25"/16 x 63.5 cm

GAUGE

28 sts x 36 rows = 4"/10 cm square
Adjust needle size if necessary to obtain gauge.

NOTES

- This stocking is worked from the top down, back and forth in rows, and then seamed up the back.
- The design is worked in intarsia.
- If desired, you may use the letter charts on pages 6 or 17 to create your own name or phrase at the top in place of "Noel," either working the letters using stranded knitting as you go or adding them at the end in duplicate stitch.

Leg

With Color A, CO 82 sts.
Rows 1–12: Knit.
Row 13 (RS): Knit.
Row 14: Purl
Rows 15–162: Continue in St st, following the chart for colors and decreasing where indicated by knitting or purling 2 sts together at the end of the row.
Row 163: Knit first 16 sts (outlined), then slip them back onto the left-hand needle and knit them again with a scrap piece of yarn in a different color. Continue across row following chart to end, then slip last 16 sts back onto

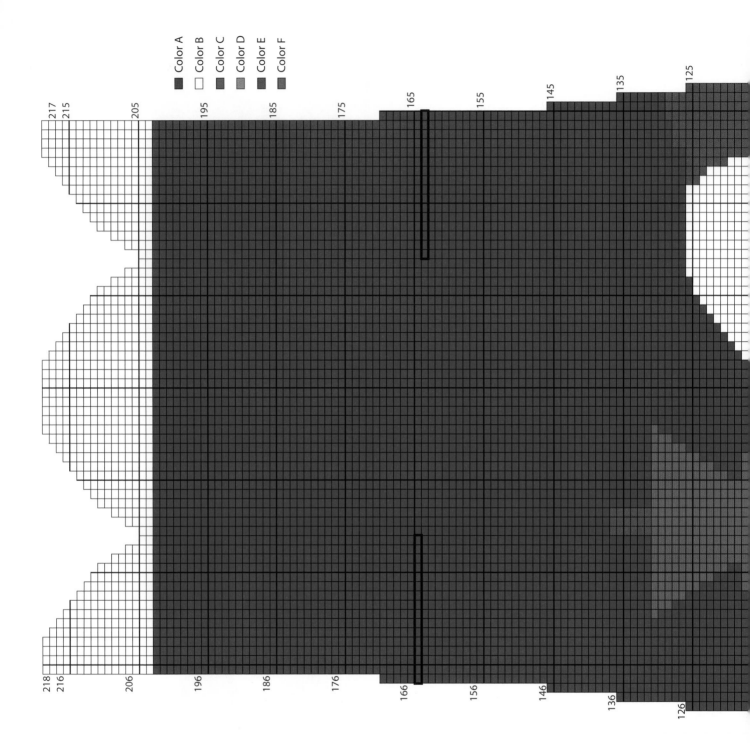

Snowman

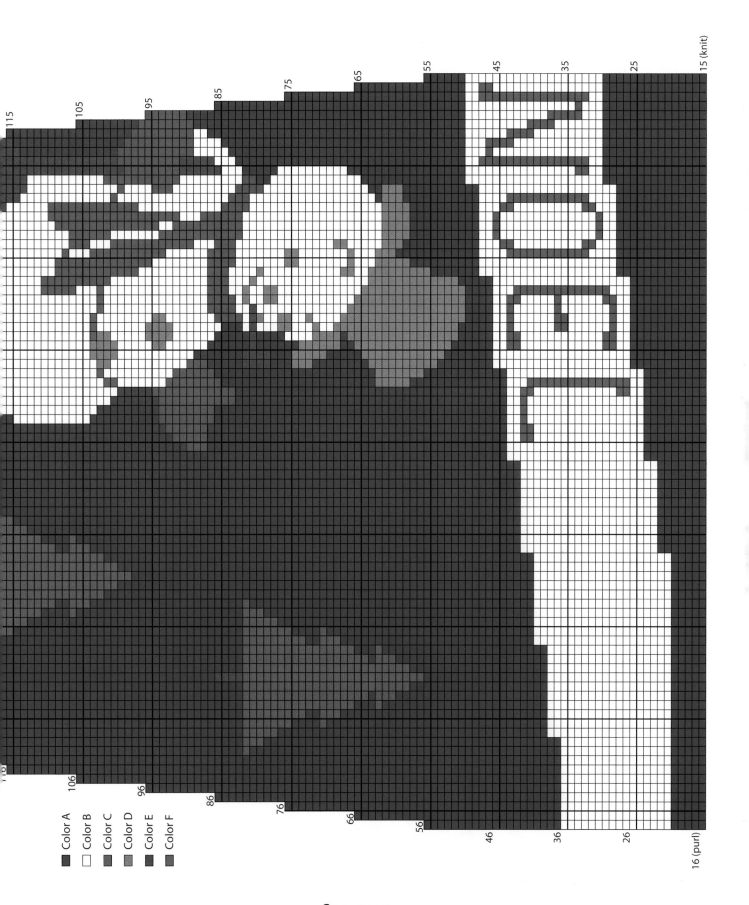

Snowman

Color A
Color B
Color C
Color D
Color E
Color F

115
105
95
85
75
65
55
45
35
25
15 (knit)

106
96
86
76
66
56
46
36
26
16 (purl)

left-hand needle and knit them again with another piece of contrasting-color yarn.

Row 164: Purl as normal across all sts, following the color chart.

Rows 165–202: Continue in St st, following the chart for colors and decrease placement.

Toe

Join Color B and break off any other colors still in use.

Row 203: Knit.

Row 204: P15, pm, p30, pm, p15.

Row 205: Knit to 3 sts before first marker, ssk, k1, sm; k1, k2tog, knit to 3 sts before second marker, ssk, k1, sm; k1, k2tog, knit to end.

Row 206: Purl.

Rows 207–210: Rep Rows 205–206.

Row 211: Rep Row 205.

Row 212: Purl to 3 sts before first marker, p2tog, p1, slip marker; p1, p2tog, purl to 3 sts before second marker, p2tog, p1, slip marker; p1, p2tog, purl to end.

Rows 213–218: Rep Rows 211–212—16 sts rem at end of Row 16.

Bind off.

Heel

Pull out the piece of scrap yarn marking the stitches for one half of the heel. Pick up 16 dropped sts along each edge of opening created, plus 2 sts on inner edge of opening—34 sts on needle.

Join Color B at right edge of sts on wrong side.

Row 1: P17, pm, p17.

Row 2: Knit to 3 sts before marker, ssk, k1, sm, k1, k2tog, knit to end.

Row 3: Purl.

Rows 4–9: Rep Rows 2–3.

Row 10: Knit to 3 sts before marker, ssk, k1, sm, k1, k2tog, knit to end—24 sts.

Row 11: Purl to 3 sts before marker, p2tog, p1, sm, p1, p2tog, purl to end—22 sts.

Repeat Rows 10–11 until 2 sts remain.

Bind off.

Repeat on other side of heel.

Finishing

With right sides facing, sew back seam of stocking. Turn right side out. Attach decorative cord or yarn for hanging.

Candy Cane Christmas

Who says Christmas has to be all red and green? Bright turquoise accents in this stocking give it a playful feel. Children will have fun finding the presents on and under the tree: a ball, candy cane, teddy bear, drum, and horn. What do you want this year?

YARN

Knit Picks Palette, fingering weight #1 yarn, (100% Peruvian Highland wool, 231 yd./211 m per 1.7 oz./50 g ball)
- 2 skeins Cream (Color A)
- 1 skein Calypso Heather (Color B)
- 1 skein Grass (Color C)
- 1 skein Pimento (Color D)
- 1 skein Mongoose (Color E)
- Small amounts of Asphalt Heather (Color F) and Cornmeal (Color G)

NEEDLES AND OTHER MATERIALS

- US 3 (3.25 mm) straight needles
- Waste yarn
- Tapestry needle
- Decorative cord or yarn for hanging
- Optional: bobbins for working intarsia

MEASUREMENTS

6 x 23"/15 x 58 cm

GAUGE

28 sts x 36 rows = 4"/10 cm square
Adjust needle size if necessary to obtain gauge.

NOTES

- This stocking is worked from the top down, back and forth in rows, and then seamed up the back.
- The design is worked in intarsia.
- As shown, the name was worked in duplicate stitch after the stocking was knitted, but you may also use the letter charts on pages 6 or 17 to create your own name or phrase in stranded knitting as you go.

Leg

With Color A, CO 82 sts.
Rows 1–12: Knit.
Row 13 (RS): Knit.
Row 14: Purl.
Rows 15–146: Continue in St st, following the chart for colors and decreasing where indicated by knitting or purling 2 sts together at the end of the row.
Row 147: Knit first 16 sts (outlined in red), then slip them back onto the left-hand needle and knit them again with

a scrap piece of yarn in a different color. Continue across row following chart to end, then slip last 16 sts back onto left-hand needle and knit them again with another piece of contrasting-color yarn.
Row 148: Purl as normal across all sts, following the color chart.
Rows 149–188: Continue in St st, following the chart for colors and decrease placement.

Toe

Join Color B and break off any other colors still in use.

Row 189: Knit.

Row 190: P15, pm, p30, pm, p15.

Row 191: Knit to 3 sts before first marker, ssk, k1, sm; k1, k2tog, knit to 3 sts before second marker, ssk, k1, sm; k1, k2tog, knit to end.

Row 192: Purl.

Rows 193–196: Rep Rows 191–192.

Row 197: Rep Row 191.

Row 198: Purl to 3 sts before first marker, p2tog, p1, slip marker; p1, p2tog, purl to 3 sts before second marker, p2tog, p1, slip marker; p1, p2tog, purl to end.

Rows 199–204: Rep Rows 197–198—16 sts rem at end of Row 204.

Bind off.

Heel

Pull out the piece of scrap yarn marking the stitches for one half of the heel. Pick up 16 dropped sts along each edge of opening created, plus 2 sts on inner edge of opening—34 sts on needle.

Join Color B at right edge of sts on wrong side.

Row 1: P17, pm, p17.

Row 2: Knit to 3 sts before marker, ssk, k1, sm; k1, k2tog, knit to end.

Row 3: Purl.

Rows 4–9: Rep Rows 2–3.

Row 10: Knit to 3 sts before marker, ssk, k1, sm; k1, k2tog, knit to end—24 sts.

Row 11: Purl to 3 sts before marker, p2tog, p1, sm, p1, p2tog, purl to end—22 sts.

Repeat Rows 10–11 until 2 sts remain.

Bind off.

Repeat on other side of heel.

Finishing

If desired, add a name in duplicate stitch to the top of the stocking, referencing one of the letter charts on pages 6 or 17. With right sides facing, sew back seam of stocking. Turn right side out. Attach decorative cord or yarn for hanging.

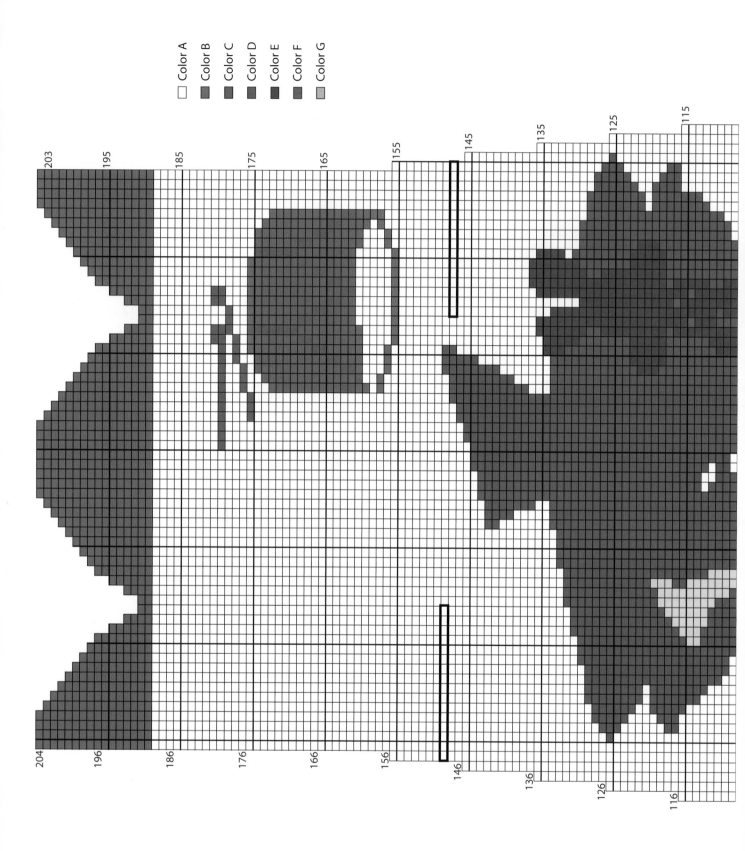

Candy Cane Christmas

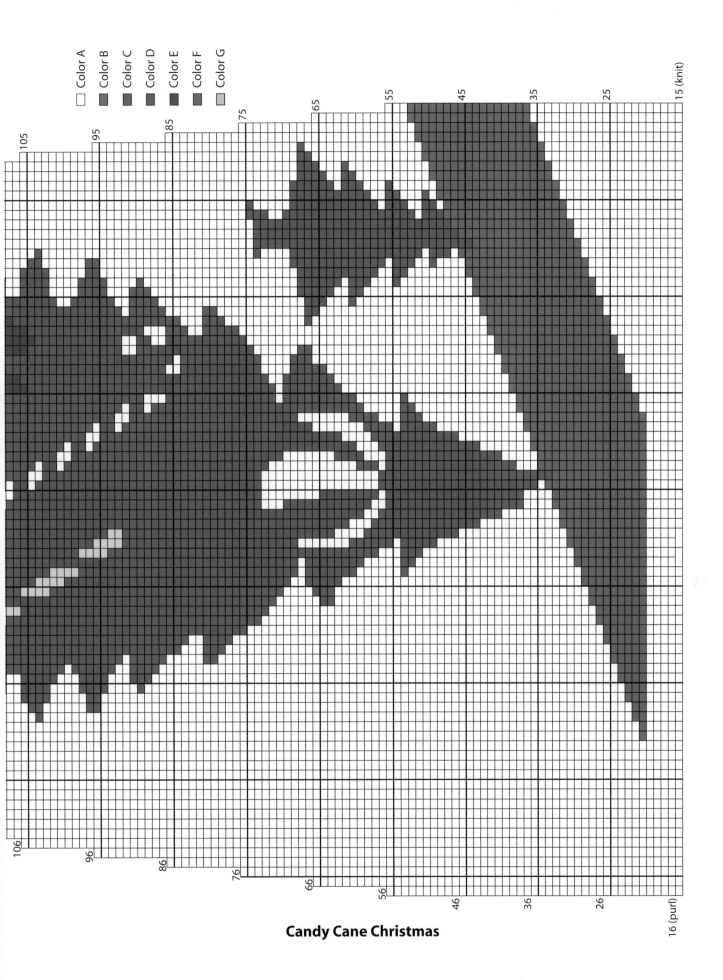

Candy Cane Christmas

Scandinavian Star Slippers

Keep your ankles and tootsies warm on Christmas morning and all winter long in these stranded knitted slippers with suede bottoms. The stranded design doubles the yarn across your instep, providing extra warmth and a nice, snug fit.

Shown in 9"/23 cm size.

YARN

Knit Picks Palette, super fine weight #1 yarn (100% Peruvian Highland wool; 231 yd./211 m per 1.7 oz./50 g ball)
- 2 (2) skeins Abyss Heather (MC)
- 1 (1) skein Finnley Heather (CC)

NEEDLES AND OTHER MATERIALS

- For 9"/23 cm size, set of US 2 (2.75 mm) double-pointed needles
- For 11–12"/28–30 cm size, US 3 (3.25 mm) double-pointed needles
- Slipper soles in appropriate size (shown in Fiber Trends Suede Slipper Soles)
- Tapestry needle

SIZES

Small (Large)
9"/23 cm (11–12"/28–30 cm)

GAUGE

For 9"/23 cm size, 7.75 sts = 1"/2.5 cm square
For 11–12"/28–30 cm size, 7 sts = 1"/2.5 cm square
Adjust needle size if necessary to obtain gauge.

STITCH GUIDE

Make 1 (M1)
Make 1 by lifting the thread before the next stitch and knitting into the back of it.

SPECIAL TECHNIQUES

Kitchener Stitch
Hold the stitches for the instep on one needle and the stitches for the sole on a second needle. Thread the yarn (about 15"/38 cm) on a tapestry needle. Hold the needle with the yarn attached farthest from you (back needle), and start on the needle nearest you (the front needle), as follows: *Insert the tapestry needle into the first stitch of the front needle as if to knit and slip this stitch off the needle. Insert the tapestry needle into the second stitch of the front needle as if to purl, and pull the yarn through but leave the stitch on the knitting needle. Go to the back needle, being careful to take the yarn under the needle each time. Insert the tapestry needle into the first stitch of the back needle as if to purl, and slip this stitch off the needle. Insert the tapestry needle through the next stitch on the back needle as if to knit, and pull the yarn through, leaving the stitch on the knitting needle. Repeat from * until all stitches are joined. Do not draw the yarn too tightly; the stitches should have the same tension as the knitted stitches. Fasten the end securely and weave it in.

NOTES

- This pattern comes in two sizes, 9"/23 cm and 11–12"/28–30 cm long. The difference in size is made by using slightly larger needles for the larger size. *Unless specified, instructions apply to both sizes.*
- Slippers are worked from the cuff down, similarly to a sock, and then the sole is sewn on after knitting is complete.

Cuff

Using MC and double-pointed needles, CO 52 sts. Divide the sts on three needles and join.
Work k2, p2 ribbing for 6"/15 cm.
Inc row: *K5, M1; repeat from * to last 2 sts, k2—62 sts.
Divide the sts as follows: 31 sts for the heel on one needle, 15 instep sts on one needle, 16 instep sts on one needle.

Heel

Working across the 31 heel sts only, k1, sl 1 across the row.
Purl back.
Repeat these two rows for 33 rows for small size (2.75"/7 cm for large size).
Turn the heel on a *purl row* as follows:
Row 1: P17, p2tog, p1, turn.
Row 2: Sl 1, k4, k2tog, k1, turn.
Row 3: Sl 1, p5, p2tog, p1, turn.
Row 4: Sl 1, k6, k2tog, k1, turn.
Continue to decrease in the same way (having one more st between the decreases after each row) until there are 17 sts left.
With the right side of the work toward you, pick up and knit 14 sts on the left side of the heel. Slip the 31 sts for the

instep onto one needle and knit across these sts. Pick up and knit 14 sts on the right side of the heel. Knit to the center of the heel.

Gusset

Divide the 45 heel sts on two needles (the 31 sts for the instep are already on one needle).

Start at the center of the heel and knit to the last 3 sts on that needle, k2tog, k1. Knit across the instep. On the last needle, k1, ssk, knit to the end of the needle.

Continue to decrease in the same way for 6 more rows—31 heel sts, 31 instep sts.

Color Chart

Now you are ready to work the Color Chart. Begin with the instep needle; read the diagram right to left. Carry the yarn loosely at the back of the work. Twist the yarn you carry around the working yarn if the yarn is carried more than three sts. Start to decrease for the toe at Row 45, working in pattern, as follows:

Instep needle: K1, sl 1, k1, psso, k to last 3 sts on the needle, k2tog, k1.

First sole needle: K2tog, knit to end of needle.

Second sole needle: Knit to last 2 sts on the needle, k2tog.

Knit 1 row.

Continue to decrease in the same way *every other* row until there are 17 sts for the instep and 17 sts for the sole. Break the yarn, leaving about 15"/38 cm of MC.

Join with Kitchener stitch.

Finishing

Press the socks lightly using a damp cloth or a steam iron.

To attach the sole to the sock, first pin the heel of the sock to the heel of the sole, matching the center backs. Do the same with the toe. Then baste the sole to the sock, following the outline of the pattern except at the gusset, where the outline comes slightly above the sole. With a yarn needle and two strands of yarn (your choice of MC or CC), sew together using blanket stitch. Remove the basting thread.

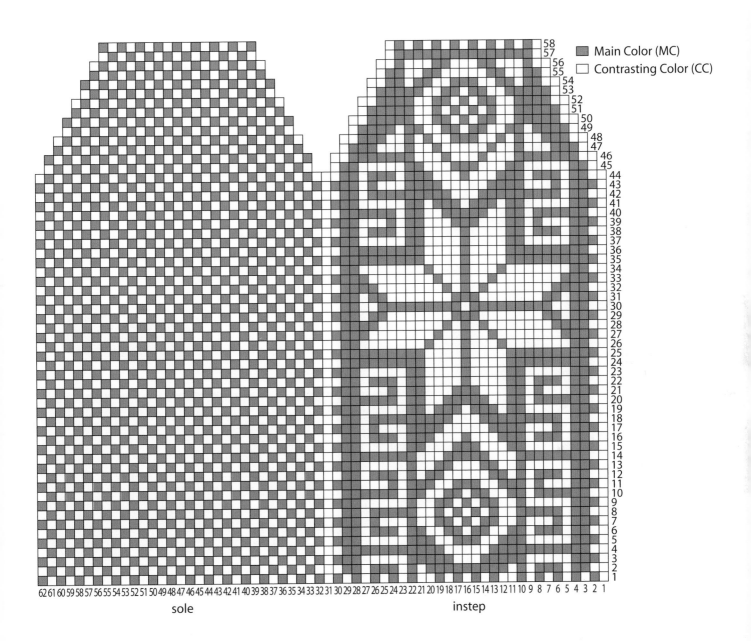

Color Chart

Children's Scandinavian Slippers

These little booties look so cute on tiny feet—or in a stocking or under a tree. They are such fast knits because of their small size you could make several pairs in a variety of colors and give a set to every toddler on your Christmas list.

Shown in size 1–2 years

YARN

Knit Picks Palette, super fine weight #1 yarn (100% Peruvian Highland wool; 231 yd./211 m per 1.7 oz./50 g ball)
- 1 skein Mist (MC)
- 1 skein Ivy (CC)

NEEDLES AND OTHER MATERIALS

- Set of US 3 (3.25 mm) double-pointed needles
- Slipper soles in appropriate size (shown in Fiber Trends Suede Slipper Soles)
- Tapestry needle

SIZES

1–2 years (4"/10 cm slipper sole)
3–4 years (6"/15 cm slipper sole)
Instructions for larger size are in parentheses.

GAUGE

8 sts x 9 rows = 1"/2.5 cm
Adjust needle size if necessary to obtain gauge.

SPECIAL TECHNIQUES

Kitchener Stitch

Hold the stitches for the instep on one needle and the stitches for the sole on a second needle. Thread the yarn (about 15"/38 cm) on a tapestry needle. Hold the needle with the yarn attached farthest from you (back needle), and start on the needle nearest you (the front needle), as follows: *Insert the tapestry needle into the first stitch of the front needle as if to knit and slip this stitch off the needle. Insert the tapestry needle into the second stitch of the front needle as if to purl, and pull the yarn through but leave the stitch on the knitting needle. Go to the back needle, being careful to take the yarn under the needle each time. Insert the tapestry needle into the first stitch of the back needle as if to purl, and slip this stitch off the needle. Insert the tapestry needle through the next stitch on the back needle as if to knit, and pull the yarn through, leaving the stitch on the knitting needle. Repeat from * until all stitches are joined. Do not draw the yarn too tightly; the stitches should have the same tension as the knitted stitches. Fasten the end securely and weave it in.

NOTES

- Slippers are worked from the cuff down, similarly to a sock, and then the sole is sewn on after knitting is complete.

Cuff

With MC and double-pointed needles, CO 36 (40) sts. Divide the stitches on three needles and join.

Work k1, p1 ribbing for 10 (12) rows, twisting the knit stitches by inserting the needle as if to purl and then knitting each stitch. The twisted knit stitches will make the ribbing firmer; twist the knit stitches for the ribbing only.

Divide the stitches as follows: 17 (19) sts for the heel on one needle, 10 (10) instep sts on one needle, and 9 (11) instep sts on one needle.

Heel

Working across heel sts only, k1, sl 1 across.
Purl back.
Repeat these 2 rows until you have 8 (10) knit-slip rows.
Turn the heel on a purl row, as follows:
Row 1: P10 (11), p2tog, p1, turn.
Row 2: Sl 1, k4, k2tog, k1, turn.
Row 3: Sl 1, p5, p2tog, p1, turn.
Row 4: Sl 1, k6, k2tog, k1, turn.
Continue to decrease in the same way, having 1 more stitch between the decreases after each row, until 11 stitches remain.

With the right side of the work toward you, pick up and knit 6 (7) sts on the left side of the heel. Slip the 19 (21) sts for the instep onto one needle and knit across these stitches. Pick up and knit 6 (7) sts on the right side of the heel. Knit to the center of the heel.

Gusset

Divide the stitches so that you have the 19 (21) sts for the instep on one needle and the 23 (24) sts for the heel on two needles. Start at the center of the heel and knit to the last 3 stitches on the needle, k2tog, k1. Knit across the instep. On the last needle, k1, ssk, knit to the end of the needle.

Repeat the decreases in the next row—19 (21) heel sts, 19 (21) instep sts.

Color Chart

Now you are ready to work the Color Chart. Make sure you follow the correct chart for the size you are making. Start with the instep needle, reading the chart from right to left. Carry the yarn loosely at the back of the work. Twist the yarn you carry around the working yarn if the yarn is carried more than 4 stitches.

Start to decrease for the toe at Row (20) 25. Work in pattern and decrease as follows:

Instep needle: K1, sl 1, k1, psso, knit to last 3 sts, k2tog, k1.
First sole needle: K2tog, knit to end of needle.
Second sole needle: Knit to last 2 sts, k2tog.
Knit 1 row.

Continue to decrease in the same way, every other row, until there are 13 stitches left for the instep and 13 stitches for the sole (both sizes). Break the yarn, leaving about 15"/38 cm of the background color.

Join the toe with Kitchener stitch.

Finishing

Press the socks lightly using a damp cloth or a steam iron.

To attach the sole to the sock, first pin the heel of the sock to the heel of the sole, matching the center backs. Do the same with the toe. Then baste the sole to the sock, following the outline of the pattern except at the gusset, where the outline comes slightly above the sole. With a tapestry needle and one strand of background yarn, sew together using blanket stitch. Remove the basting thread.

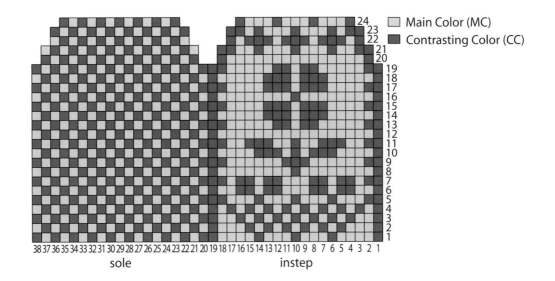

1 to 2 Year Size Color Chart

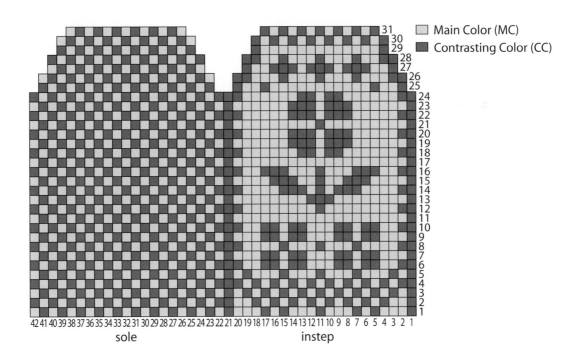

3 to 4 Year Size Color Chart

Santa Pajama Case

Perfect for sleepovers at Grandma's house on Christmas Eve, this Santa is made to carry your PJs snug in his belly—that's what will give him that nice, round look. Tuck your pajamas in and button his belt and you are ready to go. He's quite snuggly for an overnight buddy, too.

Design by Vicky Gordon/KnittingbyPost.com

Bulky weight #5 yarn
- 7 oz./200 g red
- 3.5 oz./100 g white
- 3.5 oz./100 g black
- 1.7 oz./50 g cream

NEEDLES AND OTHER MATERIALS

- US 7 (4.5 mm) needles
- Stuffing
- Large button
- Stitch marker
- Tapestry needle
- Small piece of cardboard (to make pom-pom)

MEASUREMENTS (STUFFED)

Tip of beard to top of hat: 14"/35.5 cm
Bottom of foot to top of glove: 20"/50 cm
Width at belt: 10"/25 cm

GAUGE

16 sts x 22 rows in St st = 4"/10 cm square
Adjust needle size if necessary to obtain gauge.

Arms (Make 1 Left and 1 Right)

Right

With red, CO 30 sts.
Starting with a purl row, work in St st for 7 rows.
Change to white and knit 6 rows.
Change to black. Starting with a knit row, work in St st for 6 rows.**

Split for gloves
Hand: Knit 20 sts and turn. Put remaining sts on a stitch holder.
Knit in St st for 7 rows.
Next row: *K2, k2tog; rep from * to end—15 sts.
Purl 1 row.
Next row: *K1, k2tog; rep from * to end—10 sts.
Purl 1 row.
Draw thread through the remaining stitches and pull tight.
Thumb: Reattach black yarn to remaining stitches, and work in St st for 4 rows.
Next row: K1, *k2tog; rep from * to last st, k1—6 sts.
Purl 1 row.
Draw thread through the remaining sts and pull tight.

Left

Work as per the right arm to **.
Thumb: Knit 10 sts and turn. Put remaining sts on a stitch holder.
Knit in St st for 3 rows.
Next row: K1, *k2tog; rep from * to last st, k1—6 sts.
Purl 1 row.
Draw thread through the remaining stitches and pull tight.
Hand: Reattach black yarn to remaining stitches and, starting with a knit row, work in St st for 8 rows.
Next row: *K2, k2tog; rep from * to end—15 sts.
Purl 1 row.
Next row: *K1, k2tog; rep from * to end—10 sts.
Purl 1 row.
Draw thread through the remaining sts and pull tight.
For both hands, fold the thumb in half lengthways and sew down the inner side. Fold the hand in half lengthways and sew down the inner side. Sew the remaining row ends together to form the arm, and stuff.

Legs (Make 2)

With black, CO 30 sts.
Purl 1 row.
Next row: *K1, kfb; rep from * to end—45 sts.
Starting with a purl row, work in St st for 4 rows.
Knit 1 row.
Starting with a knit row, work in St st for 8 rows.
Shape boot: K12, [k2tog] 11 times, k11—34 sts.
Purl 1 row.
Next row: K11, [k2tog] 6 times, k11—28 sts.
Starting with a purl row, knit in St st for 6 rows.
Knit 1 row.
Change to red yarn.
Next row: *K4, kfb; rep from * to last 3 sts, k3—33 sts.
Starting with a purl row, work in St st for 7 rows.
Cast off.
Sew down the row ends of the boot and along the boot's sole. Stuff the leg.

Main Body

With white, CO 86 sts.
Knit 10 rows.
Change to red yarn and, starting with a knit row, continue in St st for 18 rows, knitting the first and last 10 sts of every purl row.
Change to black yarn and knit 3 rows.
Buttonhole row: K3, k2tog, CO 2, k2tog, knit to end—86 sts.
Knit 2 rows.

Change to red yarn and continue in St st for 27 rows, knitting the first and last 10 sts of every purl row.

Cast off.

Lay the body on a table with the right side facing down. Fold the row ends of the piece so that the knitted borders overlap in the center with the buttonhole uppermost. The part facing is now the underside of the body. The white border is the bottom of Santa's coat.

Pin the piece to hold together. Attach and sew the legs to the lower part of the body. Make sure the seams of the boots are facing each other and the boot toe is facing outwards.

Attach the arms to the top of the body with the thumbs innermost to the body at a mirror image to each other and the seams of the arms facing the underside of the body.

Sew a large button to the center of Santa's belly to hold the flap closed.

Belt Buckle

With white, CO 36 sts.

Knit 1 row.

Cast off.

Sew the buckle around the button in a square shape, making sure the row ends meet.

Head

With cream, CO 15 sts.

Purl 1 row.

Next row: *Kfb; rep from * to end—30 sts.

Purl 1 row.

Next row: *K1, kfb; rep from * to end—45 sts.

Purl 1 row.

Next row: *K2, kfb; rep from * to end—60 sts.

Starting with a purl row, work in St st for 21 rows and add a stitch marker at stitch 30 of Row 13. This signifies the center of the head and where to attach the nose.

Next row: K14, k2tog, k28, k2tog, k14—58 sts.

Purl 1 row.

Next row: K12, k2tog twice, k25, k2tog twice, k13—54 sts.

Purl 1 row.

Next row: K12, k2tog twice, k23, k2tog twice, k11—50 sts.

Purl 1 row.

Next row: *K2, k2tog; rep from * to last 2 sts, k2—38 sts.

Purl 1 row.

Next row: *K1, k2tog; rep from * to last 2 sts, k2—26 sts.

Purl 1 row.

Next row: K2tog to end—13 sts.

Draw thread through remaining sts and pull tight.

Sew down the row ends of the piece and add stuffing. Then gather the cast-on stitches to seal.

Beard

With white, CO 62 sts.

Knit 4 rows.

Next row: K2tog, knit to last 2 sts, k2tog.

Repeat the previous row until 22 sts remain.

Next row: [K2tog] twice, knit to last 4 sts, [k2tog] twice.

Repeat this row twice more—10 sts.

Knit 1 row.

Cast off.

Mustache

With white, CO 6 sts.

Purl 1 row.

Next row: *Kfb; rep from * to end—12 sts.

Starting with a purl row, work in St st for 5 rows.

Next row: K4, [k2tog] twice, k4—10 sts.

Work in St st for 3 rows.

Next row: K2tog, k6, k2tog—8 sts.

Purl 1 row.

Attach the nose to the face over the stitch marker. Stitch mustache to the beard at either side of the nose. Sew two eyes in black on either side of the upper nose on the face. Go over the stitch two or three times to get the desired thickness. Sew a small mouth in black between the mustache and beard. Sew the head onto the body between the arms.

Santa Hat

With white, CO 60 sts.

Knit 10 rows.

Change to red yarn and, starting with a knit row, work in St st for 6 rows.

Next row: K1, *k2tog, k8; rep from * to last 9 sts, k2tog, k7—54 sts.

Work in St st for 5 rows.

Next row: K1, *k2tog, k7; rep from * to last 8 sts, k2tog, k6—48 sts.

Work in St st for 5 rows.

Next row: K1, *k2tog, k6; rep from * to last 7 sts, k2tog, k5—42 sts.

Work in St st for 5 rows.

Next row: K1, *k2tog, k5; rep from * to last 6 sts, k2tog, k4—36 sts.

Work in St st for 5 rows.

Next row: K1, *k2tog, k4; rep from * to last 5 sts, k2tog, k3—30 sts.

Work in St st for 5 rows.

Next row: K1, *k2tog, k3; rep from * to last 4 sts, k2tog, k2—24 sts.

Work in St st for 5 rows.

Next row: K1, *k2tog, k2; rep from * to last 3 sts, k2tog, k1—18 sts.

Work in St st for 5 rows.

Next row: K1, *k2tog, k1; rep from * to last 2 sts, k2tog—12 sts.

Work in St st for 5 rows.

Next row: K2tog to end—6 sts.

Work in St st for 5 rows.

Next row: K2tog to end—3 sts.

Draw thread through remaining sts and pull tight.

Sew down the row ends to make the hat shape.

Pom-Pom

Make a pom-pom by wrapping yarn around a small rectangle of cardboard many times. Slide a short piece of yarn between the yarn wraps and the cardboard and tie it tightly, gathering the yarn as closely as possible. Then cut through all of the yarn wraps opposite the tie to complete the pom-pom. Trim as desired. Sew to the pointed end of the hat.

Next row: K2tog, k4, k2tog—6 sts.

Purl 1 row.

Next row: K2tog to end—3 sts.

Draw thread through the remaining sts and pull tight.

Fold mustache in half lengthways and sew down the row ends.

Nose

With cream, CO 3 sts.

Next row: Kfb, k1, kfb—5 sts.

Starting with a purl row, work in St st for 3 rows.

Next row: K2tog, k1, k2tog—3 sts.

Cast off.

Pass thread through the outer edges and gather and pull tight to form a button-shaped nose.

Attach the beard around Santa's head with the cast-on stitches uppermost and the widest part meeting at the back of the head. Use the stitch marker to place the top of the beard in the correct position on the face.

Colorwork Ornaments

Often the most treasured ornaments are those made by hand—ours or someone else's. We remember those ones particularly, when they were made and by whom, and we relive the memories each year when we hang those ornaments. These colorwork ornaments are sure to become some of your family's favorites.

The colorwork designs in these ornaments were inspired by Sanquhar knitting, a distinctive two-colored patterned knitting that takes its name from the small city of Sanquhar, located in the south of Scotland in Dumfries and Galloway. Traditionally knit in black and white wool in intricate geometric patterns, the ornaments included here have been modified and worked in a variety of colors.

Four different cap styles—Solid, Salt and Pepper, Striped, and Ring—are presented for use with the narrow band patterns #1–13. Charts for #14–18 are for use with the Solid Cap with Wide Pattern ornament. By mixing and matching colors and charts, you can make a variety of ornaments and have none of them be exactly alike.

Design by Amy Munson

YARN

Knit Picks Palette, fingering weight #1 yarn (100% Peruvian Highland wool; 231 yd./211 m per 1.7 oz./50 g ball)
- Two colors, approx. 2 yd./1.8 m of each

NEEDLES AND OTHER MATERIALS

- US 1 (2.25 mm) set of 5 double-pointed needles
- 4 stitch markers
- Stuffing
- Crochet hook
- Tapestry needle
- Optional: hemostats (for stuffing ornament)

MEASUREMENTS

Circumference: 7.75"/20 cm
Diameter: 2.5"/6 cm

GAUGE

9 sts in St st in the round = 1"/2.5 cm
Adjust needle size if necessary to obtain gauge.

NOTES

- All of the ornament patterns are written and charted. Ornaments are knit in the round and the charts are designed to be read from the bottom to the top, right to left for all rounds.
- Charts #1–13 for the Pattern Rounds—Rounds 13–27— can be interchanged in any of the narrow pattern band cap styles (Solid, Salt and Pepper, Stripe, and Ring).
- Charts #14–18 are for use with the Solid Cap Ornament with Wide Pattern.
- A variety of increase and decrease stitches are used to create each ornament and they change depending on the cap pattern. The written pattern will specify what stitch to use and when.
- Stitch markers can be used to keep track of the colorwork pattern repeats. Place one marker between each pattern repeat that is mid-needle. The first marker is placed after stitch 10, the second after stitch 20, stitch 30 will happen at the end of a needle so no need for a marker, one more after stitch 40, and the last marker after stitch 50. Having the markers in place helps keep the pattern repeats easy to follow.
- To finish an ornament, cut the working yarn leaving an extra-long tail and pull the tail through remaining stitches. Block, then stuff the ornament. Finally, weave in the ends

using the tapestry needle, taking care to close up the top and bottom holes. I like to weave in the ends after the ornament is stuffed. It is a little easier to hide them in the stuffing as well as use them to shape the ornament. Use the extra-long tail to crochet a 5"/13 cm chain and form a loop to hang the ornament.
- To block, soak ornament in cool water until completely saturated, then remove from bath and squeeze out any excess water. An additional squeeze in a towel will remove most of the excess moisture. Lay as flat as possible and allow ornament to dry completely before stuffing.
- To achieve a nice, round ornament, fluff up the stuffing and then push it into the ornament. Be careful not to wad it up as it is inserted as this will result in lumps. A pair of hemostats is a great help to get the stuffing down the small hole.
- If you notice a stitch done in the wrong color, don't rip back. Simply finish up the ornament, block and stuff it, and then go back and change the offending stitch with a duplicate stitch of the correct color.

Solid Cap Ornament

Solid Cap in Rose pattern #1 with Contrast Color for cap (left) and Solid Cap in Rose pattern #1 with Main Color for cap (right)

CO 12 sts and split evenly over 4 needles (choose either the MC or the CC to be the cap color). Join to work in the round.

Increases

Rnd 1: Knit.
Rnd 2: [Kfb, knit to last st on needle, kfb] rep on each needle—20 sts.
Rnds 3, 5, 7, 9, 11: Knit.
Rnd 4: [K1, kfb, knit to last 2 sts on needle, kfb, k1] rep on each needle—28 sts.
Rnd 6: [K1, kfb, knit to last 2 sts on needle, kfb, k1] rep on each needle—36 sts.
Rnd 8: [K1, kfb, knit to last 2 sts on needle, kfb, k1] rep on each needle—44 sts.
Rnd 10: [K1, kfb, knit to last 2 sts on needle, kfb, k1] rep on each needle—52 sts.
Rnd 12: [K1, kfb, knit to last 2 sts on needle, kfb, k1] rep on each needle—60 sts.

Pattern Rounds

Rnds 13–27: Follow chart for selected pattern #1–#13.

Solid Cap in Cross pattern #9

Decreases

Note: Change to cap color if necessary.

Rnd 28 and all even rounds to end: Knit.

Rnd 29: [K1, ssk, knit to last 2 sts on needle, k2tog, k1] rep on each needle—52 sts.

Rnd 31: [K1, ssk, knit to last 2 sts on needle, k2tog, k1] rep on each needle—44 sts.

Rnd 33: [K1, ssk, knit to last 2 sts on needle, k2tog, k1] rep on each needle—36 sts.

Rnd 35: [K1, ssk, knit to last 2 sts on needle, k2tog, k1] rep on each needle—28 sts.

Rnd 37: [K1, ssk, knit to last 2 sts on needle, k2tog, k1] rep on each needle—20 sts.

Rnd 39: [Ssk, knit to last 2 sts on needle, k2tog] rep on each needle—12 sts.

Follow instructions for finishing in Notes on page XX.

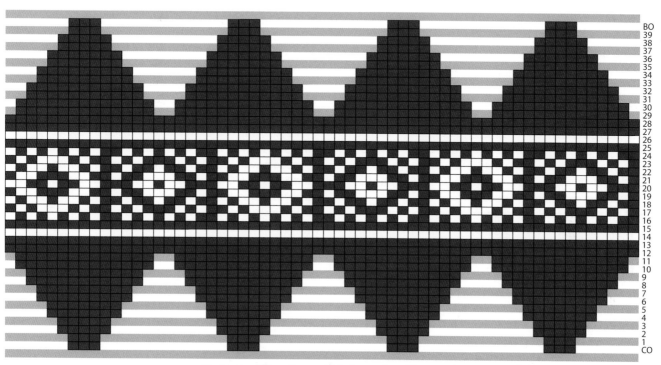

Pattern #1 – Rose (Main color for cap)

Pattern #1 – Rose (Contrast color for cap)

Salt and Pepper Cap Ornament

CO 12 sts in MC, split evenly onto 4 needles and join to work in the round.

Increases

Rnd 1: [K1, kfb, k1] rep on each needle—16 sts.
Rnd 2: Knit.
Rnd 3: [With MC M1, (with CC k1, with MC k1) to end of needle, with CC M1] rep on each needle—24 sts.
Rnds 4, 6, 8, 10, 12: Knit in pattern around.
Rnd 5: [With CC M1, knit in pattern across needle, with MC M1] rep on each needle—32 sts.
Rnd 7: [With MC M1, knit in pattern across needle, with CC M1] rep on each needle—40 sts.
Rnd 9: [With CC M1, knit in pattern across needle, with MC M1] rep on each needle—48 sts.
Rnd 11: [With MC M1, knit in pattern across needle, with CC M1] rep on each needle—56 sts.

Pattern Rounds

Rnds 13–27: Follow chart for selected pattern #1–#13, increasing in Rnd 13 by M1 at the beginning of each needle—60sts.

Decreases

Rnd 28: [With CC k2tog, (with MC k1, with CC k1) across needle] rep on each needle—56 sts.
Rnd 29 and all odd rnds to end: Knit all sts in pattern around.
Rnd 30: [With MC k2tog, knit in pattern to last 2 sts on needle, with CC ssk] rep on each needle—48 sts.
Rnd 32: [With CC k2tog, knit in pattern to last 2 sts on needle, with MC ssk] rep on each needle—40 sts.
Rnd 34: [With MC k2tog, knit in pattern to last 2 sts on needle, with MC ssk] rep on each needle—32 sts.
Rnd 36: [With CC k2tog, knit in pattern to last 2 sts on needle, with MC ssk] rep on each needle—24 sts.
Rnd 38: With MC [k2tog, k2, ssk] rep on each needle—16 sts.
Rnd 40: [K2tog, k2] rep on each needle—12 sts.
Follow instructions for finishing in Notes on page 67.

Pattern #2 – Duke

Stripe Cap Ornament

With CC, CO 12 sts and split evenly over 4 needles. Join to work in the round.

Increases

Rnd 1: [With CC k1, with MC k1, with CC k1] rep on each needle.

Rnd 2: [With MC M1, knit in Stripe pattern across needle, with MC M1] rep on each needle—20 sts.

Rnds 3, 5, 7, 9, 11: Knit all sts in pattern.

Rnd 4: [With CC M1, knit in pattern to last st on needle, with CC M1] rep on each needle—28 sts.

Rnd 6: [With MC M1, knit in pattern to last st on needle, with MC M1] rep on each needle—36 sts.

Rnd 8: [With CC M1, knit in pattern to last st on needle, with CC M1] rep on each needle—44 sts.

Rnd 10: [With MC M1, knit in pattern to last st on needle, with MC M1] rep on each needle—52 sts.

Rnd 12: [With CC M1, knit in pattern to last st on needle, with CC M1] rep on each needle—60 sts.

Pattern Rounds

Rnds 13–27: Follow chart for selected pattern #1–#13.

Decreases

Rnd 28: [With CC k1, with MC k1] rep across needle ending with a CC st.

Rnd 29: [With MC k2tog, knit in pattern to last 2 sts on needle, with MC ssk] rep on each needle—52 sts.

Rnd 30 and all even rnds through Rnd 38: Knit all sts in stripe pattern.

Rnd 31: [With CC k2tog, knit in pattern to last 2 sts on needle, with CC ssk] rep on each needle—44 sts.

Rnd 33: [With MC k2tog, knit in pattern to last 2 sts on needle, with MC ssk] rep on each needle—36 sts.

Rnd 35: [With CC k2tog, knit in pattern to last 2 sts on needle, with CC ssk] rep on each needle—28 sts.

Rnd 37: [With MC k2tog, knit in pattern to last 2 sts on needle, with MC ssk] rep on each needle—20 sts.

Rnd 39: [With CC k2tog, knit in pattern to last 2 sts on needle, with CC ssk] rep on each needle—12 sts.

Rnd 40: With CC knit.

Follow instructions for finishing in Notes on page 67.

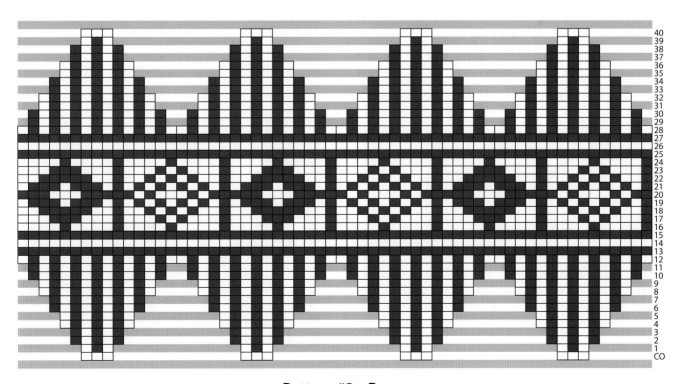

Pattern #3 – Rose

Salt and Pepper Cap in Duke pattern #2 (left) and Ring Cap in Drum pattern #4 (right)

Stripe Cap in Rose pattern #3

Stripe Cap in Rose pattern #3 (top) and Solid Cap in wide Checked pattern #17

Ring Cap Ornament

CO 12 sts with CC and split evenly over 4 needles. Join to work in the round.

Increases

Rnd 1: With CC knit.

Rnd 2: [With CC k1, M1, knit to last st on needle, M1, k1] rep on each needle—20 sts.

Rnds 3, 5, 7, 9, 11: With MC knit.

Rnd 4: [With CC k1, M1, knit to last st on needle, M1, k1] rep on each needle—28 sts.

Rnd 6: [With CC k1, M1, knit to last st on needle, M1, k1] rep on each needle—36 sts.

Rnd 8: [With CC k1, M1, knit to last st on needle, M1, k1] rep on each needle—44 sts.

Rnd 10: [With CC k1, M1, knit to last st on needle, M1, k1] rep on each needle—52 sts.

Rnd 12: [With MC k1, M1, knit to last st on needle, M1, k1] rep on each needle—60 sts.

Pattern Rounds

Rnds 13–27: Follow chart for selected pattern #1–#13.

Decreases

Rnd 28: With MC knit.

Rnd 29: [With MC k1, ssk, knit to last 3 sts on needle, k2tog, k1] rep on each needle—52 sts.

Rnd 30 and all even rnds through Rnd 40: With CC knit.

Rnd 31: [With MC k1, ssk, knit to last 3 sts on needle, k2tog, k1] rep on each needle—44 sts.

Rnd 33: [With MC k1, ssk, knit to last 3 sts on needle, k2tog, k1] rep on each needle—36 sts.

Rnd 35: [With MC k1, ssk, knit to last 3 sts on needle, k2tog, k1] rep on each needle—28 sts.

Rnd 37: [With MC ssk, knit to last 2 sts on needle, k2tog] rep on each needle—20 sts.

Rnd 39: [With CC ssk, k1, k2tog] rep on each needle—12 sts.

Follow instructions for finishing in Notes on page 67.

Ring Cap in Drum pattern #4

Pattern #4 – Drum

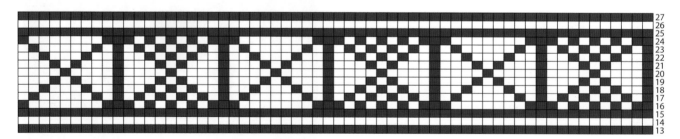

Pattern #5 – Drum & Trellis

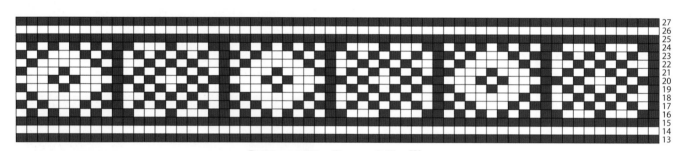

Pattern #6 – Cornet

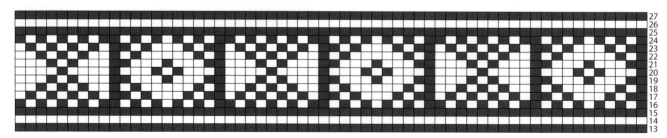

Pattern #7 – Cornet & Drum

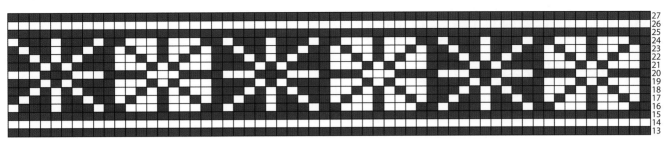

Pattern #9 – Cross

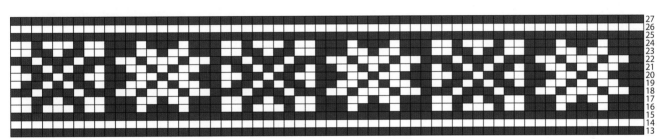

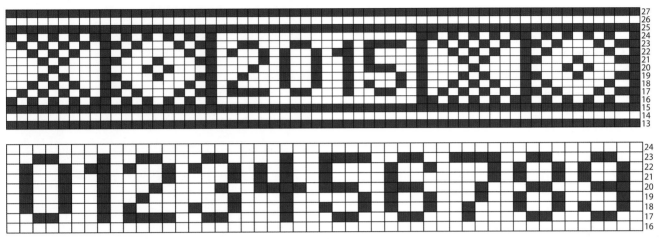

Pattern #10 – Happy New Year

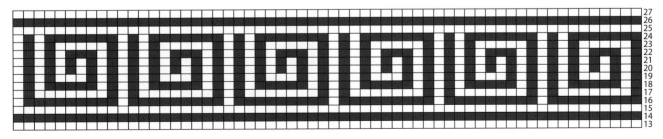

Pattern #11 – Snowflake

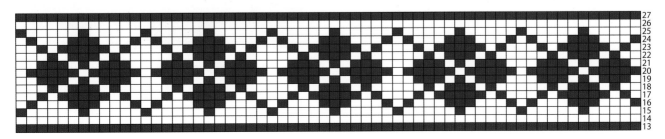

Pattern #12 – Roman Key

Pattern #13 – Argyle

Solid Cap Ornament with Wide Pattern

CO 12 sts in MC and split evenly over 4 needles. Join to work in the round.

Increases

Rnd 1: Knit.
Rnd 2: [Kfb, knit to last st on needle, kfb] rep on each needle—20 sts.
Rnds 3, 5, 7, 9, 11: Knit.
Rnd 4: [K1, kfb, knit to last 2 sts on needle, kfb, k1] rep on each needle—28 sts.
Rnd 6: [K1, kfb, knit to last 2 sts on needle, kfb, k1] rep on each needle—36 sts.
Rnd 8: [K1, kfb, knit to last 2 sts on needle, kfb, k1] rep on each needle—44 sts.
Rnd 10: [K1, kfb, knit to last 2 sts on needle, kfb, k1] rep on each needle—52 sts.

Pattern Rounds

Rnd 12: [With CC k1, M1, knit to last 2 sts on needle, M1, k1] rep on each needle—60 sts.
Rnds 13–28: Follow chart for selected pattern #14–#18.

Decreases

Rnd 29: [With MC k1, ssk, knit to last 2 sts on needle, k2tog, k1] rep on each needle—52 sts.
Rnd 30 and all even rnds through Rnd 40: Knit.
Rnd 31: [K1, ssk, knit to last 2 sts on needle, k2tog, k1] rep on each needle—44 sts.
Rnd 33: [K1, ssk, knit to last 2 sts on needle, k2tog, k1] rep on each needle—36 sts.
Rnd 35: [K1, ssk, knit to last 2 sts on needle, k2tog, k1] rep on each needle—28 sts.
Rnd 37: [K1, ssk, knit to last 2 sts on needle, k2tog, k1] rep on each needle—20 sts.
Rnd 39: [Ssk, k1, k2tog] rep on each needle—12 sts.
Follow instructions for finishing in Notes on page 67.

Solid Cap in wide Shepherd's Plaid pattern #14

Solid Cap in wide Boxed pattern #18

Pattern #14 – Shepherd's Plaid

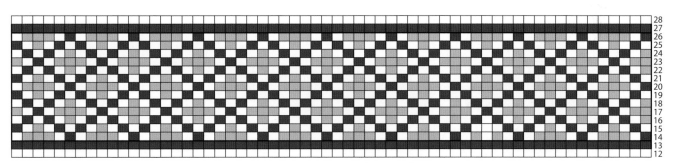

Pattern #15 – Midge & Flea

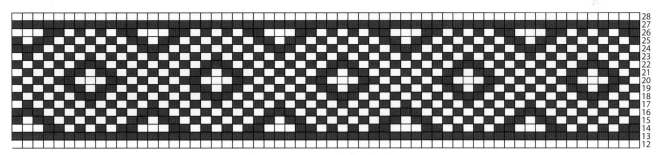

Pattern #16 – Fleur De Lys

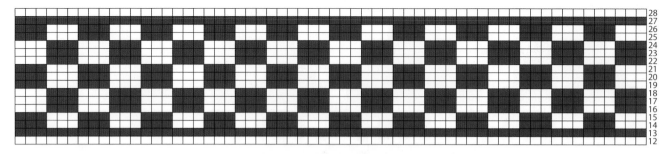

Pattern #17 – Checked

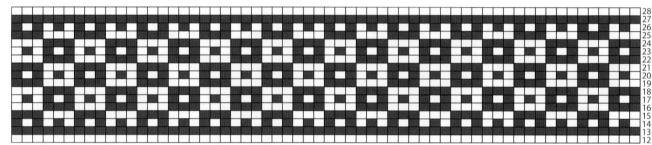

Pattern #18 – Boxed

Solid Cap in wide Fleur De Lys pattern #16 (left) and Solid Cap in Rose pattern #1 with Contrast Color for cap (right)

At right: Solid Cap in Happy New Year pattern #10

Stormy Dawn
Hobby Horse

Stormy Dawn is the fastest hobby horse in town. A simple pattern knit in the round, it is very similar to a sock. The ears are also knit in the round, which enables them to stand straight up, and the only seaming is stitching them to the head. The bridle, eyes, and mane can be customized using any materials you like.

Design by Sara Elizabeth Kellner/Rabbit Hole Knits

YARN

Medium weight #4 yarn, in any colors you choose
- Approx. 150 yd./137 m for head
- Approx. 5 yd./4.5 m for mane
- Approx. 10 yd./9 m for bridle

NEEDLES AND OTHER MATERIALS

- Set of four US 4 (3.5 mm) double-pointed needles
- Tapestry needle
- 3 stitch markers
- Stuffing
- Small book rings or other metal rings for bridle (optional)
- ³/₄"/2 cm wooden dowel, about 1 yd./1 m long
- 1 upholstery nail or other small nail with a wide head
- Embroidery thread, buttons, felt, or other embellishment for eyes
- Fabric glue (optional)

MEASUREMENTS (STUFFED)

Neck to nose: 13.5"/34 cm
Width: 6"/15 cm

GAUGE

18 sts x 28 rows in St st = 4"/10 cm square
Adjust needle size if necessary to obtain gauge.

STITCH GUIDE

Sl 1, K1, Psso
Slip 1 st, knit 1 st, then pass the slipped stitch over the knitted stitch.

Pick Up & Knit (PU)
Working right to left, insert the needle from front to back where you want to add the stitch, wrap the yarn around the needle knitwise and pull through to the front of the fabric. Repeat until you have picked up as many stitches as called for in the pattern.

Head

Begin at neck.
CO 24 sts onto 3 dpns (8 sts on each needle) and join to work in the round.
Work in k2, p2 rib for 2"/5 cm.
Then work the following rounds:
Rnd 1: Knit.
Rnd 2: *K2, kfb; rep from * to end of rnd—32 sts.

Rnds 3–4: Knit.
Rnd 5: *K3, kfb; rep from * to end of rnd—40 sts.
Rnds 6–7: Knit.
Rnd 8: *K3, kfb; rep from * to end of rnd—50 sts.
Rnds 9–10: Knit.
Rnd 11: *K4, kfb; rep from * to end of rnd—60 sts.
Knit all sts for an additional 5"/13 cm.
Rearrange the stitches so that the first 15 from needle 1 and the last 15 from needle 3 are on one dpn, and the middle 30 sts are on a second dpn. Work back and forth on the front dpn in St st (K the RS and P the WS), decreasing 1 st on each end (ssk on the right side; k2tog on the left side) of the RS rows until 20 sts remain.
On the next RS row begin the following:
Row 1: K12, sl 1, k1, psso, turn work.
Row 2: P5, p2tog, turn work.
Row 3: K5, sl 1, k1, psso, turn work.
Row 4: P5, p2tog, turn work.
Repeat Rows 3–4 five more times until 6 sts remain. This part of the horse's head will be referred to as the "heel" from here on in this pattern, since it is just like knitting the heel of a sock.
Knit across the heel, then PU 15 sts on the left side of it. Knit all 30 sts on the second dpn. PU 15 sts on the other side of heel. Arrange the sts so that there are 22 on each dpn. Knit all sts for 1.5"/4 cm.
Then work the following rounds:
Rnd 1: *K11, pm, k11; rep from * on each dpn.
Rnd 2: *K9, ssk, sm, k2tog, k9; rep from * on each dpn—60 sts.
Rnds 3–10: Knit.
Rnd 11: *K8, ssk, sm, k2tog, k8; rep from * on each dpn—54 sts.
Rnds 12–19: Knit.
Rnd 20: *K7, ssk, sm, k2tog, k7; rep from * on each dpn—48 sts.
Rnds 21–28: Knit.
Rnd 29: *K6, ssk, sm, k2tog, k6; rep from * on each dpn—42 sts.
Rnds 30–31: Knit.
Rnd 32: *K2tog; rep from * to end of rnd—21 sts.
Rnd 33: Knit.
Rnd 34: *K2tog; rep from * to last st in round, k1—11 sts.
Rnd 35: Knit.
Rnd 36: *K2tog; rep from * to last st in round, k1—6 sts.
Cut yarn and thread through remaining live sts. Pull tightly closed and insert yarn needle down through center of nose to secure end.
Stuff body firmly through the opening at neck. The wooden dowel or a straight knitting needle can help.

After stuffing, insert the wooden dowel up through the center of the horse's neck until it reaches the heel at the top of the head. This is where the end of the dowel will rest. Hammer an upholstery nail down through the horse's forehead and into the center of the dowel. It will be covered up by the mane.

Ear (Make 2)

CO 18 sts (6 on each dpn).
Rnds 1–2: Knit.
Rnd 3: *K1, kfb, k1, kfb, k2; rep from * on each dpn.
Knit all sts for an additional 1"/2.5 cm.
Rnd 4: *K2, k2tog, k2, k2tog; rep from * on each dpn.
Rnds 5–6: Knit.
Rnd 7: *K1, k2tog, k1, k2tog; rep from * on each dpn.
Rnds 8–9: Knit.
Rnd 10: *K2tog twice; rep from * on each dpn.
Rnd 11: Knit.
Cut yarn, thread through remaining live sts, insert needle down through center of ear and secure end to the inside. Make another ear exactly the same. Ears should be seamed to the head about .5"/1.25 cm in on each side of the heel.

Mane

Cut about 30 pieces of yarn 6"/15 cm long. You can make your horse's mane thicker or thinner if you like. Thread each piece on a yarn needle and slip under a stitch along the back of the horse's head, beginning between the ears and running down to almost the end of its head. After each piece of yarn is in place with 3"/7.5 cm on each side, tie a knot to secure it. Trim if desired.

Bridle

The bridle is made from a 4-stitch I-cord, which was ironed slightly on a low setting to make it flatter. Four separate pieces are needed (refer to photos for placement):
• One the circumference of the horse's nose
• One the circumference of the head just below the ears
• Two short ones which will extend between the others
Use book rings or any other metal rings (if desired) on the sides of the bridle. To secure the bridle to the horse's head, it can be stitched or glued with fabric glue.

Eyes

Eyes can be made out of anything you choose. For the horse pictured, a small piece of white felt was glued in place and a black button sewn on top.

Santa Booties

These fluffy red and white booties will be just the shoes to go with your little girl's first Christmas dress. They'll be knitted in a wink!

Design by Alma Mahler/Heaven to Seven

YARN

DK weight baby yarn
• 1.7 oz./50 g red
Eyelash or other fluffy yarn
• Small amount of white

NEEDLES AND OTHER MATERIALS

• US 5 (3.75 mm) needles
• Tapestry needle
• Small piece of cardboard for making pom-poms

SIZE/MEASUREMENTS

Size: 3 to 9 months
Sole: 4"/10 cm

GAUGE

22 sts x 28 rows = 4"/10 cm square
Adjust needle size if necessary to obtain gauge.

STITCH GUIDE

Make 1 (M1)
Make 1 by picking up the strand between two stitches and knitting into it.

Sole

The sole is worked in garter stitch, which means you knit all rows.
With red yarn, CO 33 sts.
Row 1: Knit.
Row 2: K2, M1, k14, M1, k1, M1, k14, M1, k2—37 sts.
Row 3: Knit.
Row 4: K2, M1, k16, M1, k1, M1, k16, M1, k2—41 sts.
Row 5: Knit.
Row 6: K2, M1, k18, M1, k1, M1, k18, M1, k2—45 sts.
Row 7: Knit.
Continue to increase in this way 2 more times until you have 53 sts.
Leave red yarn attached and knit 2 rows of garter st using the eyelash yarn. Cut eyelash yarn. This completes the sole.
Now continue in St st (knit RS, purl WS), working 2 rows.

Shape Upper

Next row: K24, k2tog, k1, ssk, k24—51 sts.
Next row: Purl.
Next row: K23, k2tog, k1, ssk, k23—49 sts.
Next row: Purl.
Next row: K22, k2tog, k1, ssk, k22—47 sts.
Next row: Purl.
Continue decreasing in this manner 5 more times, until 37 sts remain and ending with a purl row.
Work 6 rows of St st without further shaping. Cut red yarn.
Work 2 rows of garter stitch using white eyelash yarn.
BO all stitches.

Finishing

Sew up the sole and center back seams using mattress stitch. Weave in all ends.
With red wool, make two twisted cords, as follows: Cut 2 strands of yarn 31.5"/80 cm long. Knot the strands together at each end and insert a pencil through one end. Pin down the other end securely. Keeping the yarn full length and taut, twist the pencil until the yarn is tightly twisted and kinks when the tension is relaxed. Fold yarn in half keeping it taut to avoid tangling and remove pencil. Make a knot at both ends, leaving extra yarn to attach pom-poms.
Make small pom-poms about 1"/2.5 cm diameter. Make a pom-pom by wrapping yarn around a small rectangle of cardboard many times. Slide a short piece of yarn between the yarn wraps and the cardboard and tie it tightly, gathering the yarn as closely as possible. Then cut through all of the yarn wraps opposite the tie to complete the pom-pom. Trim as desired.
With a tapestry needle, thread the cords through the tops of the booties about 1"/2.5 cm below the top. Attach pom-poms securely.
Make another bootie the same way.

Woodland Wreath

There are all sorts of things to be found nestling amongst the leaves of this wreath: flowers, berries—even a knitted creature or two. The wreath is first covered with knitting and then layers of different leaves and decorations are added until it's full to bursting.

I've made two sizes of the wreath and most of the twelve project patterns come in two sizes so that you can choose one to match the size of your wreath. Many of the pieces could also be used to decorate other things or just made on their own as fun gifts. A family of hedgehogs, anyone?

This wreath is great for using up stash and leftover bits of yarn. I've listed the yarns and needle sizes I have used, but feel free to substitute and use what you have on hand. Gauge is not critical for most of these pieces, so substitution is easy; just use a needle size that complements your chosen yarn, and you are ready to knit.

Design by Frankie Brown/Frankie's Knitted Stuff

WREATH

• •

The wreaths I used are made of polystyrene; they have flat backs and are available in various sizes. I chose two and then designed two sizes of decorations, one for each wreath (see Measurements for the wreath sizes I used). This means there should be patterns suitable for whatever size wreath you find. You may also, of course, choose to use both sizes of decorations on one wreath.

The cover is knitted flat in sections and then sewn together on the wreath. This is less boring than knitting one huge cover and it ensures that it will fit. It is no fun at all to have to unravel a strip of knitting with hundreds of stitches after finding it's the wrong size. If your wreath is a different size than mine, measure the circumference and knit the first section to fit. It can be tried on the wreath as you go. Then just keep adding strips until you have covered the wreath.

I knitted mine in green, but it doesn't matter much what color you use as most of the cover will be hidden by the leaves and decorations.

YARN

Stylecraft Special DK, light weight #3 yarn (100% acrylic; 322 yd./295 m per 3.5 oz./100 g skein)
• Bottle, 1 skein for large wreath, 1.7 oz./50 g for small wreath

NEEDLES AND OTHER MATERIALS

• US 6 (4 mm) needles
• Polystyrene wreath in any size
• Tapestry needle

MEASUREMENTS

Big wreath
External diameter: 13.75"/35 cm
Internal diameter: 7.5"/19 cm
Circumference: 9"/23 cm
Small wreath
External diameter: 9.75"/25 cm
Internal diameter: 5.5"/14 cm
Circumference: 6.25"/16 cm

GAUGE

16 sts x 16 rows in k1, p1 rib = 2"/5 cm square
Gauge is not critical, as long as it fits your wreath. The rib allows a good deal of stretch.

Large and small polystyrene wreaths with flat backs

Cover for the Big Wreath

Using the long-tail method, CO 40 sts.

Work 70 rows in k1, p1 rib.

Cast off in rib, leaving a long tail.

Wrap the knitted strip around the wreath and sew the cast-on and cast-off ends together. You can hide this join on the back of the wreath. Work four more strips in the same way, sewing each on to the wreath as you go. Use mattress stitch to join the strips, matching up the seams on the back of the wreath. It might not look as though five strips will be enough, but knitting stretches.

Should you want to knit the cover all in one (and, if so, you're a braver knitter than I), you will need to work 70 rows of k1, p1 rib on 200 sts.

The entire wreath is covered.

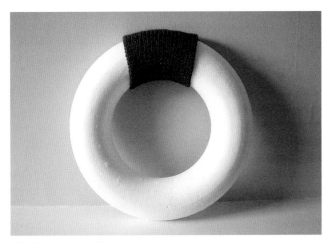

The first strip is knitted and sewn on.

Cover for the Small Wreath

This is worked in the same way as the bigger cover. Work strips of k1, p1 rib on 40 sts, but this time only work 45 rows.

You will need four of these strips to cover the wreath.

Alternatively, knit 45 rows of k1, p1 rib on 160 sts.

Attach Hanging Ring

You will need to sew a small ring to the back of your wreath to hang it up. I used curtain rings, .75"/20 mm for the big wreath and .5"/15 mm for the small. Attach them quite low down on the back to allow for the knitting pulling up when the wreath is hung.

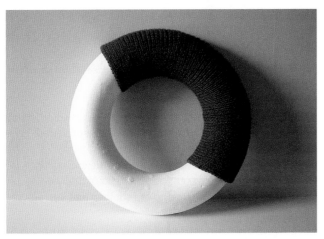

Knit and add more strips the same way, seaming cast-on and bound-off edges together and connecting to previous strip with mattress stitch.

Add a ring or other hanging device to the back of the wreath.

LEAVES

• •

After covering the wreath, the first thing to add is a layer of basic leaves. This will form the backdrop to all the other decorations. The leaves are knitted with DK weight yarn; you can use one yarn or oddments of lots of shades of green as each leaf is knitted separately. The stems of the leaves are worked in I-cord while the leaves are knitted back and forth.

You can make all big leaves for a large wreath and all small leaves for a small wreath, or mix the two sizes on one wreath. First you knit the leaves, then join in a garland before attaching to the wreath.

YARN

Stylecraft Vision DK, light weight #3 yarn (80% acrylic, 20% wool; 308 yd./282 m per 3.5 oz./100 g skein)
• #1498 Greensleeves, 1 skein for the large wreath, 1.7 oz./ 50 g for the small wreath

NEEDLES AND OTHER MATERIALS

• Two US 5 (3.75 mm) double-pointed needles
• Tapestry needle

MEASUREMENTS

Big leaf: 2.75"/7 cm long (excluding stem)
Small leaf: 2"/5 cm long (excluding stem)

GAUGE

Gauge is not critical.

STITCH GUIDE

Slip 1 (sl 1)
In this pattern, slip stitches purlwise with the yarn in front.
Slip 2, Knit, Pass Slipped Stitches Over (S2KP2)
Slip 2 sts as if to knit them together, knit 1 st, and pass slipped stitches over—2 sts decreased.

SPECIAL TECHNIQUES

Cable Cast-On
Make a slip knot and place it on the left-hand needle. Knit a stitch but do not pull it off the left-hand needle; instead transfer the new stitch from right to left needle, leaving two stitches on the left-hand needle. *Now insert the needle between the two stitches, wrap the yarn around the needle as if to knit, and pull the yarn through. Transfer

A big leaf and a small leaf

the newly created stitch onto the left-hand needle. Repeat from * until you have the number of stitches needed.
I-Cord
Knit every row but don't turn the work at the ends of the rows. Slide the stitches to the other end of the needle, pull the yarn around from behind the stitches, and knit again.

Big Leaf (Make 60 for the Large Wreath)

Note: All slipped stitches should be slipped purlwise with the yarn held at the front of the work.
Using the long-tail method, CO 3 sts.
Work 10 rows in I-cord for the stem.
Now slide the stitches to the end of the needle, as if you were going to carry on in I-cord, and CO 8 more sts using the cable cast-on, working into the back loop only for the first stitch and then through both loops as normal after that.
Row 1: Knit—11 sts.

Row 2: CO 8 sts, k8, p1, sl 1, p1, k8—19 sts.
Row 3: Kfb, k7, S2KP2, k8—18 sts.
Row 4: Kfb, k7, sl 1, k9—19 sts.
Row 5: K8, S2KP2, k8—17 sts.
Row 6: K8, sl 1, k8.
Row 7: Kfb, k6, S2KP2, k7—16 sts.
Row 8: Kfb, k6, sl 1, k8—17 sts.
Row 9: K7, S2KP2, k7—15 sts.
Row 10: K7, sl 1, k7.
Row 11: K6, S2KP2, k6—13 sts.
Row 12: K6, sl 1, k6.
Row 13: K5, S2KP2, k5—11 sts.
Row 14: K5, sl 1, k5.
Row 15: K4, S2KP2, k4—9 sts.
Row 16: K4, sl 1, k4.
Row 17: K3, S2KP2, k3—7 sts.
Row 18: K3, sl 1, k3.
Row 19: K2, S2KP2, k2—5 sts.
Row 20: K2, sl 1, k2.
Row 21: K1, S2KP2, k1—3 sts.
Row 22: K1, sl 1, k1.

Work one more S2KP2 and fasten off. Weave the end in down the vein on the underneath of the leaf but leave the cast-on tail for joining the leaves.

I'll tell you how to knit the small leaves next and then explain how to join them together.

Small Leaf

(Make 40 for the Small Wreath)

Note: All slipped stitches should be slipped purlwise with the yarn held at the front of the work.

Using the long-tail method, CO 3 sts.

Work 8 rows in I-cord.

Now slide the stitches to the end of the needle, as if you were going to carry on in I-cord, and CO 6 more sts using the cable cast-on, working into the back loop only for the first stitch and then through both loops as normal after that.

Row 1: Knit—9 sts.
Row 2: CO 6 sts, k6, p1, sl 1, p1, k6—15 sts.
Row 3: Kfb, k5, S2KP2, k6—14 sts.
Row 4: Kfb, k5, sl 1, k7—15 sts.
Row 5: K6, S2KP2, k6—13 sts.
Row 6: K6, sl 1, k6.
Row 7: Kfb, k4, S2KP2, k5—12 sts.
Row 8: Kfb, k4, sl 1, k6—13 sts.
Row 9: K5, S2KP2, k5—11 sts.
Row 10: K5, sl 1, k5.
Row 11: K4, S2KP2, k4—9 sts.
Row 12: K4, sl 1, k4.
Row 13: K3, S2KP2, k3—7 sts.
Row 14: K3, sl 1, k3.
Row 15: K2, S2KP2, k2—5 sts.
Row 16: K2, sl 1, k2.
Row 17: K1, S2KP2, k1—3 sts.
Row 18: K1, sl 1, k1.

Work one more S2KP2 on the remaining 3 sts and finish off in the same way as for the big leaf.

Joining the Leaves

The leaves will be joined together into one long garland. This is done in the same way for both the big and the small leaves.

Use the cast-on tail to sew the stem of the new leaf to the side of the previous leaf. Sew it to the top of the first leaf's stem and finish before you get to the top of the stem on the new leaf (you may need to read this sentence a few times). Add the leaves to the garland as you make them, sewing them alternately to the left and right sides of the previous leaf.

I knitted 60 leaves for the big wreath and 40 for the small one. You could also mix the sizes within your garland. When you feel like you never want to see another leaf again, let alone knit one, it's probably time to sew your garland to the wreath.

Sew the stem of the new leaf to the side of the previous leaf.

Continue to add leaves to the garland, sewing them alternately to the left and right sides of the previous leaf.

The garland is ready to attach to the wreath.

Attaching the Leaf Garland to the Wreath

Lay the wreath on a flat surface and arrange the garland around it. Work in a zigzag, leaving the back of the wreath bare. Adjust the garland to get an even coverage and then pin it in place. If you use pins with colored heads they will be easier to find. Don't worry about the gaps—there are lots more things to come to fill those.

Now sew the garland to the wreath. Work along the stems in running stitch, taking the pins out as you go.

Arrange the garland over the wreath, pin it in place, and sew it on.

The small and large wreaths with leaves attached.

OAK LEAVES AND ACORNS

The next leaves for the Woodland Wreath are two sizes of oak leaves, each with their own acorns. To make a change from all that green, these are autumnal oak leaves, knitted in brown.

YARN

Leaves: Sirdar Click DK, light weight #3 yarn (70% acrylic, 30% wool; 164 yd./150 m per 1.7 oz./50 g skein)
- #0120, .7 oz./20 g will make 8 big leaves, .35 oz./10 g will make 8 small leaves

Acorn nuts: Rowan Felted Tweed, light weight #3 yarn (50% merino wool, 25% alpaca, 25% rayon; 191 yd./175 m per 1.7 oz./50 g skein)
- Small amount #160

Acorn cups: Stylecraft Special DK, light weight #3 yarn (100% acrylic; 322 yd./295 m per 3.5 oz./100 g skein)
- Small amount Mocha

NEEDLES AND OTHER MATERIALS

- Two US 5 (3.75 mm) double-pointed needles
- Two US 2 (2.75 mm) needles
- Tapestry needle
- Small amount of stuffing material

MEASUREMENTS

Big oak leaf: 3.5"/9 cm long
Small oak leaf: 3"/8 cm long

GAUGE

Gauge is not critical.

STITCH GUIDE

Make 1 (M1)
Make 1 by lifting the thread before the next stitch and knitting into the back of it.

Slip 1 (sl 1)
In this pattern, slip stitches purlwise with the yarn in front.

Slip 2, Knit, Pass Slipped Stitches Over (S2KP2)
Slip 2 sts as if to knit them together, knit 1 st, and pass slipped stitches over—2 sts decreased.

SPECIAL TECHNIQUES

Cable Cast-On
Make a slip knot and place it on the left-hand needle. Knit a stitch but do not pull it off the left-hand needle; instead transfer the new stitch from right to left needle, leaving two stitches on the left-hand needle. *Now insert the needle between the two stitches, wrap the yarn around the needle as if to knit, and pull the yarn through. Transfer the newly created stitch onto the left-hand needle. Repeat from * until you have the number of stitches needed.

I-Cord
Knit every row but don't turn the work at the ends of the rows. Slide the stitches to the other end of the needle, pull the yarn around from behind the stitches, and knit again.

Big Oak Leaf (Make 8)

Note: All slipped stitches should be slipped purlwise with the yarn held at the front of the work.

Using the long-tail method and US 5 (3.75 mm) needles, CO 3 sts.

Work 4 rows in I-cord.

Now slide the stitches to the end of the needles, as if you were going to carry on in I-cord, and CO 8 more sts using the cable cast-on, working into the back loop only for the first stitch and then through both loops as normal after that.

Row 1: Knit—11 sts.
Row 2: CO 8 sts, k8, p1, sl 1, p1, k8—19 sts.
Row 3: Kfb, k7, S2KP2, k8—18 sts.
Row 4: Kfb, k7, sl 1, k9—19 sts.
Row 5: K8, S2KP2, k8—17 sts.
Row 6: K8, sl 1, k8.
Row 7: BO 1, k5, S2KP2, k7—14 sts.
Row 8: BO 1, k5, sl 1, k6—13 sts.
Row 9: CO 3, k8, S2KP2, k5—14 sts.
Row 10: CO 3, k8, sl 1, k8—17 sts.
Row 11: Kfb, k6, S2KP2, k7—16 sts.
Row 12: Kfb, k6, sl 1, k8—17 sts.
Row 13: K7, S2KP2, k7—15 sts.
Row 14: K7, sl 1, k7.

Row 15: BO 1, k4, S2KP2, k6—12 sts.
Row 16: BO 1, k4, sl 1, k5—11 sts.
Row 17: CO 3, k7, S2KP2, k4—12 sts.
Row 18: CO 3, k7, sl 1, k7—15 sts.
Row 19: K6, S2KP2, k6—13 sts.
Row 20: K6, sl 1, k6.
Row 21: K5, S2KP2, k5—11 sts.
Row 22: K5, sl 1, k5.
Row 23: BO 1, k2, S2KP2, k4—8 sts.
Row 24: BO 1, k2, sl 1, k3—7 sts.
Row 25: K2, S2KP2, k2—5 sts.
Row 26: K2, sl 1, k2.
Row 27: Knit.
Row 28: Knit.
Row 29: K3, k2tog—4 sts.
Row 30: K2, k2tog—3 sts.
Row 31: K1, k2tog—2 sts.
K2tog and fasten off. Weave in the end down the center of the leaf but leave the cast-on end to sew the leaf to the wreath.

Small Oak Leaf (Make 8)

Note: All slipped stitches should be slipped purlwise with the yarn held at the front of the work.

Using the long-tail method and US 5 (3.75 mm) needles, CO 3 sts.

Work 4 rows in I-cord.

Now slide the stitches to the end of the needles, as if you were going to carry on in I-cord, and CO 6 more sts using the cable cast-on, working into the back loop only for the first stitch and then through both loops as normal after that.

Row 1: Knit—9 sts.
Row 2: CO 6 sts, k6, p1, sl 1, p1, k6—15 sts.
Row 3: Kfb, k5, S2KP2, k6—14 sts.
Row 4: Kfb, k5, sl 1, k7—15 sts.
Row 5: K6, S2KP2, k6—13 sts.

Row 6: K6, sl 1, k6.
Row 7: BO 1, k3, S2KP2, k5—10 sts.
Row 8: BO 1, k3, sl 1, k4—9 sts.
Row 9: CO 3, k6, S2KP2, k3—10 sts.
Row 10: CO 3, k6, sl 1, k6—13 sts.
Row 11: Kfb, k4, S2KP2, k5—12 sts.
Row 12: Kfb, k4, sl 1, k6—13 sts.
Row 13: K5, S2KP2, k5—11 sts.
Row 14: K5, sl 1, k5.
Row 15: BO 1, k2, S2KP2, k4—8 sts.
Row 16: BO 1, k2, sl 1, k3—7 sts.
Row 17: CO 2, k4, S2KP2, k2—7 sts.
Row 18: CO 2, k4, sl 1, k4—9 sts.
Row 19: K3, S2KP2, k3—7 sts.
Row 20: K3, sl 1, k3.
Row 21: K2, S2KP2, k2—5 sts.
Row 22: K2, sl 1, k2.
Row 23: K3, k2tog—4 sts.
Row 24: K2, k2tog—3 sts.
Row 25: K1, k2tog—2 sts.
K2tog and fasten off.

Acorns (Make 12 in Each Size)

Although there are two sizes of acorns, there is not much difference between them. The instructions below are for the smaller size, with variations for the larger size in parentheses. I made twelve acorns in each size, three for each pair of leaves.

Acorn Nut

Using the long-tail method and US 2 (2.75 mm) needles, CO 6 sts.

Row 1: Purl.
Row 2: [K1, M1, k1] 3 times—9 sts.
Now work 7 (9) rows in St st, beginning with a purl row.
Next row: [K1, k2tog] 3 times—6 sts.
Next row: Purl.

Big and small oak leaves

Small and large acorns

Cut the yarn, thread through the remaining sts and join the side seam, stuffing the acorn as you go. A knitting needle is useful here to push the stuffing in. Gather the cast-on end and fasten off. If you then thread the end through to the other end of the acorn and fasten it off tightly, it will flatten one end slightly for the top.

Acorn Cup

With US 2 (2.75 mm) needles, cast on 1 st, leaving a long tail for sewing the acorn to the wreath.
Knit into the front and back of this stitch—2 sts.
Row 1: Knit.
Row 2: Purl.
Row 3: Kfb, k1—3 sts.
Row 4: Purl.
Row 5: [Kfb] 3 times—6 sts.

Row 6: Purl.
Row 7: [K1, M1, k1] 3 times—9 sts.
Row 8: Purl.
Row 9: *K1, [M1, k1] twice; rep from * twice more—15 sts.
Continue for the bigger size only:
Row 10: Purl.
Row 11: Knit.
BO knitwise.
Wrap the cup around the acorn and join the ends of the cast-off row. Now sew to the acorn with running stitches worked below the cast-off row and then close the side seam.
Pin the oak leaves in pairs to the wreath and then use the cast-on tails to sew them in place along the center. Use a running stitch and stop before the top of the leaf so that it can curl. Add the acorns in groups of three.

Sew the oak leaves to the wreath in pairs and add the acorns in groups of three.

IVY

• •

Another pattern for green leaves, this time strings of ivy. As before, there are two sizes of ivy leaves but, just for a change, they are used together rather than separately. Instead of sewing individual leaves or pairs of leaves to the wreath, these are joined into short strings with three small and two big leaves on each. You could knit separate leaves if you prefer.

YARN

Rowan Felted Tweed, light weight #3 yarn (50% merino wool, 25% alpaca, 25% rayon; 191 yd./175 m per 1.7 oz./50 g skein)
• 1 skein #187

NEEDLES AND OTHER MATERIALS

• US 5 (3.75 mm) double-pointed needles
• Tapestry needle

MEASUREMENTS

Big ivy leaf: 2.75"/7 cm (excluding the stem)
Small ivy leaf: 2.25"/6 cm (excluding the stem)

GAUGE

Gauge is not critical.

STITCH GUIDE

Slip 1 (sl 1)
In this pattern, slip stitches purlwise with the yarn in front.
Slip 2, Knit, Pass Slipped Stitches Over (S2KP2)
Slip 2 sts as if to knit them together, knit 1 st, and pass slipped stitches over—2 sts decreased.

SPECIAL TECHNIQUES

Cable Cast-On
Make a slip knot and place it on the left-hand needle. Knit a stitch but do not pull it off the left-hand needle; instead transfer the new stitch from right to left needle, leaving two stitches on the left-hand needle. *Now insert the needle between the two stitches, wrap the yarn around the needle as if to knit, and pull the yarn through. Transfer the newly created stitch onto the left-hand needle. Repeat from * until you have the number of stitches needed.

Sew big and small ivy leaves together to form strings of leaves.

I-Cord
Knit every row but don't turn the work at the ends of the rows. Slide the stitches to the other end of the needle, pull the yarn around from behind the stitches, and knit again.

Small Ivy Leaf

Note: All slipped stitches should be slipped purlwise with the yarn held at the front of the work.
Begin with a small leaf on a long stem. The other four leaves will be joined on to this.
Using the long-tail method, CO 3 sts.
Work 30 rows in I-cord or until the stem is about 4"/10 cm long.
Now slide the stitches to the end of the needle, as if you were going to carry on in I-cord, and CO 7 more sts using the cable cast-on, working into the back loop only for the first stitch and then through both loops as normal after that.
Row 1: Knit—10 sts.
Row 2: CO 7 sts, k7, p1, sl 1, p1, k7—17 sts.
Row 3: Kfb, k6, S2KP2, k7—16 sts.

Row 4: Kfb, k6, sl 1, k8—17 sts.
Row 5: CO 2, BO 3, k5, S2KP2, k7—14 sts.
Row 6: CO 2, BO 3, k5, sl 1, k6—13 sts.
Row 7: K5, S2KP2, k5—11 sts.
Row 8: K5, sl 1, k5.
Row 9: Kfb, k3, S2KP2, k4—10 sts.
Row 10: Kfb, k3, sl 1, k5—11 sts.
Row 11: K4, S2KP2, k4—9 sts.
Row 12: K4, sl 1, k4.
Row 13: Kfb, k2, S2KP2, k3—8 sts.
Row 14: Kfb, k2, sl 1, k4—9 sts.
Row 15: K3, S2KP2, k3—7 sts.
Row 16: K3, sl 1, k3.
Row 17: K2, S2KP2, k2—5 sts.
Row 18: K2, sl 1, k2.
Row 19: K1, S2KP2, k1—3 sts.
Row 20: K1, sl 1, k1.
Work one last S2KP2 and fasten off. Weave in the cast-off end down the middle of the leaf.
Knit two more small leaves in the same way but with only ten rows of I-cord for the stems.

Big Ivy Leaf

Note: All slipped stitches should be slipped purlwise with the yarn held at the front of the work.
Now knit two big leaves.
Using the long-tail method, CO 3 sts.
Work 10 rows in I-cord.
Now slide the stitches to the end of the needle, as if you were going to carry on in I-cord, and CO 9 more sts.
Row 1: Knit—12 sts.
Row 2: CO 9 sts, k9, p1, sl 1, p1, k9—21 sts.

Row 3: Kfb, k8, S2KP2, k9—20 sts.
Row 4: Kfb, k8, sl 1, k10—21 sts.
Row 5: CO 2, BO 3, k7, S2KP2, k9—18 sts.
Row 6: CO 2, BO 3, k7, sl 1, k8—17 sts.
Row 7: K7, S2KP2, k7—15 sts.
Row 8: K7, sl 1, k7.
Row 9: K6, S2KP2, k6—13 sts.
Row 10: K6, sl 1, k6.
Row 11: Kfb, k4, S2KP2, k5—12 sts.
Row 12: Kfb, k4, sl 1, k6—13 sts.
Row 13: K5, S2KP2, k5—11 sts.
Row 14: K5, sl 1, k5.
Row 15: Kfb, k3, S2KP2, k4—10 sts.
Row 16: Kfb, k3, sl 1, k5—11 sts.
Row 17: K4, S2KP2, k4—9 sts.
Row 18: K4, sl 1, k4.
Row 19: K3, S2KP2, k3—7 sts.
Row 20: K3, sl 1, k3.
Row 21: K2, S2KP2, k2—5 sts.
Row 22: K2, sl 1, k2.
Row 23: K1, S2KP2, k1—3 sts.
Row 24: K1, sl 1, k1.
Work one more S2KP2 and fasten off.
To make up the string of leaves, sew one big leaf to the bottom of the main stem and a small leaf halfway up on the same side. Then add the two remaining leaves in between these on the other side of the stem, the bigger one nearest the bottom of the stem.
I made seven strands of ivy altogether, three for the small wreath and four for the big.
The ivy is useful for filling gaps amongst the leaves. Pin the strings in place and then sew them down along the stems and partway up the center of the leaves.

I added three strands of ivy to the small wreath and four to the big one.

Holly

• •

The holly leaves for the wreath are knitted separately.

YARN

Leaves: Rowan Felted Tweed, light weight #3 yarn (50% merino wool, 25% alpaca, 25% rayon; 191 yd./175 m per 1.7 oz./50 g skein)
- #158, approx. .88 oz./25 g for 12 big leaves, .5 oz./15 g for 12 small leaves

Berries: Stylecraft Special DK, light weight #3 yarn (100% acrylic; 322 yd./295 m per 3.5 oz./100 g skein)
- Small amount Claret

NEEDLES AND OTHER MATERIALS

- Two US 5 (3.75 mm) needles
- Tapestry needle

MEASUREMENTS

Big holly leaf: 3.5"/9 cm long
Small holly leaf: 2.75"/7 cm long

GAUGE

Gauge is not critical.

STITCH GUIDE

Slip 1 (sl 1)
In this pattern, slip stitches purlwise with the yarn in front.

Slip 2, Knit, Pass Slipped Stitches Over (S2KP2)
Slip 2 sts as if to knit them together, knit 1 st, and pass slipped stitches over—2 sts decreased.

SPECIAL TECHNIQUES

Cable Cast-On
Make a slip knot and place it on the left-hand needle. Knit a stitch but do not pull it off the left-hand needle; instead transfer the new stitch from right to left needle, leaving two stitches on the left-hand needle. *Now insert the needle between the two stitches, wrap the yarn around the needle as if to knit, and pull the yarn through. Transfer the newly created stitch onto the left-hand needle. Repeat from * until you have the number of stitches needed.

Big and small holly leaves. Make a variety of big and small berries to add to your holly.

I-Cord
Knit every row but don't turn the work at the ends of the rows. Slide the stitches to the other end of the needle, pull the yarn around from behind the stitches, and knit again.

NOTES

- Throughout the pattern, cast on stitches with the cable method and bind off stitches knitwise.

Big Leaf (Make 12)

Note: The slipped stitches should be slipped purlwise with the yarn held at the front of the work.
Begin at the top of the leaf.
CO 1 st and knit into the front and back of it—2 sts.
Row 1: Kfb, k1—3 sts.
Row 2: Knit.
Row 3: CO 4, BO 2, p2, k1, p1—5 sts.
Row 4: CO 4, BO 2, k2, sl 1, k3—7 sts.
Row 5: CO 4, BO 2, p4, k1, p3—9 sts.
Row 6: CO 4, BO 2, k4, sl 1, k5—11 sts.
Row 7: CO 4, BO 2, p6, k1, p5—13 sts.
Row 8: CO 4, BO 2, k6, sl 1, k7—15 sts.
Row 9: CO 4, BO 2, p7, S2KP2, p6.
Row 10: CO 4, BO 2, k7, sl 1, k8—17 sts.

Row 11: CO 3, BO 2, p7, S2KP2, p7—16 sts.
Row 12: CO 3, BO 2, k7, sl 1, k8—17 sts.
Row 13: P7, S2KP2, p7—15 sts.
Row 14: K7, sl 1, k7.
Row 15: CO 2, BO 2, p5, S2KP2, p6—13 sts.
Row 16: CO 2, BO 2, k5, sl 1, k6.
Row 17: P5, S2KP2, p5—11 sts.
Row 18: K5, sl 1, k5.
Row 19: CO 3, BO 2, p4, S2KP2, p4—10 sts.
Row 20: CO 3, BO 2, k4, sl 1, k5—11 sts.
Row 21: P4, S2KP2, p4—9 sts.
Row 22: K4, sl 1, k4.
Row 23: P3, S2KP2, p3—7 sts.
Row 24: K3, sl 1, k3.
Row 25: P2, S2KP2, p2—5 sts.
Row 26: K2, sl 1, k2.
Row 27: P1, S2KP2, p1—3 sts.
Row 28: K1, sl 1, k1.
Work one final S2KP2 and fasten off, leaving a long tail to sew the leaf to the wreath.

The knit side is the right side of the leaf. Fold the bottom of the leaf in half with the right sides together and oversew as far as the first set of spikes. Thread the tail back to the bottom of the stalk. Weave in the cast-on end on the wrong side of the leaf.

Small Leaf (Make 12)

Note: All slipped stitches should be slipped purlwise with the yarn held at the front of the work.

Begin at the top of the leaf.

Cast on 1 st and knit into the front and back of it—2 sts.

Row 1: Kfb, k1—3 sts.
Row 2: Knit.
Row 3: CO 4, BO 2, p2, k1, p1—5 sts.
Row 4: CO 4, BO 2, k2, sl 1, k3—7 sts.
Row 5: CO 4, BO 2, p4, k1, p3—9 sts.
Row 6: CO 4, BO 2, k4, sl 1, k5—11 sts.
Row 7: CO 4, BO 2, p5, S2KP2, p4.
Row 8: CO 4, BO 2, k5, sl 1, k6—13 sts.
Row 9: P5, S2KP2, p5—11 sts.
Row 10: K5, sl 1, k5.
Row 11: CO 3, BO 2, p4, S2KP2, p4—10 sts.
Row 12: CO 3, BO 2, k4, sl 1, k5—11 sts.
Row 13: P4, S2KP2, p4—9 sts.
Row 14: K4, sl 1, k4.
Row 15: CO 2, BO 2, p2, S2KP2, p3—7 sts.
Row 16: CO 2, BO 2, k2, sl 1, k3.
Row 17: P2, S2KP2, p2—5 sts.
Row 18: K2, sl 1, k2.
Row 19: P1, S2KP2, p1—3 sts.
Row 20: K1, sl 1, k1.
Work one final S2KP2 and fasten off, leaving a long tail to sew the leaf to the wreath.

The knit side is the right side of the leaf. Fold the bottom of the leaf in half with the right sides together and oversew as far as the first set of spikes. Thread the tail back to the bottom of the stalk. Weave in the cast-on end on the wrong side of the leaf.

Holly Berries

Again, these are knitted in two sizes. If you don't want to knit lots of little berries (I made 24 in each size), you could replace them with red beads.

Big Berry (Make 24)

CO 1 st and knit into the front and back of it—2 sts.
Row 1: Pfb, p1—3 sts.
Row 2: Kfb, k2—4 sts.
Row 3: Pfb, p3—5 sts.
Row 4: K3, k2tog—4 sts.
Row 5: P2, p2tog—3 sts.
Bind off with a double decrease bind-off: sl 1 knitwise, k2tog, and pass the slipped st over. Cut the yarn, leaving a long tail for sewing to the wreath. Weave in the cast-on end, then gather around the edge of the shape with the bound-off end and pull tight to make a ball.

Small Berry (Make 24)

CO 1 st and knit into the front and back of it—2 sts.
Row 1: Pfb, p1—3 sts.
Row 2: Knit.
Row 3: Purl.
Bind off with a double decrease bind-off: sl 1 knitwise, k2tog, and pass the slipped st over. Cut the yarn, leaving a long tail for sewing to the wreath. Weave in the cast-on end, then gather around the edge of the shape with the bound-off end and pull tight to make a ball.

Pin the holly leaves to the wreath in pairs. Use the cast-on tails to sew them in place along the center of the leaf, stopping before the end. Sew the berries to the bottom of the leaves, four for each pair of leaves.

Sew holly leaves to the wreath in pairs with four berries to each pair.

MISTLETOE

The last leaves for the wreath are mistletoe. These are made in pairs; how about a bunch of knitted mistletoe hung in a strategic place? Or sewn to a hat if you really have no subtlety at all?

YARN

Leaves: Rowan Felted Tweed, light weight #3 yarn (50% merino wool, 25% alpaca, 25% rayon; 191 yd./175 m per 1.7 oz./50 g skein)
• 1 skein #161
Berries: Stylecraft Special DK, light weight #3 yarn (100% acrylic; 322 yd./295 m per 3.5 oz./100 g skein)
• Small amount Cream

NEEDLES AND OTHER MATERIALS

• Two US 5 (3.75 mm) double-pointed needles
• Tapestry needle

MEASUREMENTS

Big mistletoe: 2.75"/7 cm long
Small mistletoe: 2"/5 cm long

GAUGE

Gauge is not critical.

SPECIAL TECHNIQUES

Cable Cast-On
Make a slip knot and place it on the left-hand needle. Knit a stitch but do not pull it off the left-hand needle; instead transfer the new stitch from right to left needle, leaving two stitches on the left-hand needle. *Now insert the needle between the two stitches, wrap the yarn around the needle as if to knit, and pull the yarn through. Transfer the newly created stitch onto the left-hand needle. Repeat from * until you have the number of stitches needed.

I-Cord
Knit every row but don't turn the work at the ends of the rows. Slide the stitches to the other end of the needle, pull the yarn around from behind the stitches, and knit again.

Wrap & Turn (w&t)
Short rows are used to shape the leaves. These are worked in pairs, or ridges. To prevent holes appearing when the work is turned, the following stitch should be wrapped.

Big and small mistletoe leaves, with berries attached to the large leaves

This is abbreviated as **w&t** and should be worked as follows:
Bring the yarn forward, slip the next stitch purlwise, take the yarn back again, replace the slipped stitch on the left-hand needle, bring the yarn forward again and turn the work.

NOTES

• When the pattern calls for stitches to be cast on at the start of rows, the cable cast-on should be used.

Big Leaf (Make 8)

Using the long-tail method, CO 3 sts.
Work 4 rows in I-cord.
Next row: (Still working I-cord) k1, k2tog—2 sts.
Now, pulling the yarn around as if working I-cord, CO 15 stitches at the beginning of the next row and then work in short-row ridges (each ridge is 2 short rows):
Ridge 1: K5, w&t, k5.
Ridge 2: K10, w&t, k10.
Ridge 3: K5, w&t, k5.

BO 15 sts, slipping the first stitch knitwise, k1—2 sts.

CO 15 stitches at the start of the next row for the second leaf and rep Ridges 1–3.

BO all sts, slipping the first st as before.

Sew the bottom of the second leaf to the base of the first.

Small Leaf (Make 8)

Using the long-tail method, CO 3 sts.

Work 4 rows in I-cord.

Next row: (Still working I-cord) k1, k2tog—2 sts.

Now, pulling the yarn around as if working I-cord, CO 12 sts at the beginning of the next row and then work in short-row ridges:

Ridge 1: K4, w&t, k4.

Ridge 2: K8, w&t, k8.

Ridge 3: K4, w&t, k4.

BO 12 sts, slipping the first st knitwise, k1—2 sts.

CO 12 sts at the start of the next row for the second leaf and rep Ridges 1–3.

BO all sts, slipping the first st as before.

Sew the bottom of the second leaf to the base of the first.

Berries

These are knitted in two sizes. If you don't want to knit lots of little berries (I made 16 in each size), you could replace them with cream beads.

Big Berry (Make 16)

CO 1 st and knit into the front and back of it—2 sts.

Row 1: Pfb, P1—3 sts.

Row 2: Kfb, k2—4 sts.

Row 3: Pfb, p3—5 sts.

Row 4: K3, k2tog—4 sts.

Row 5: P2, p2tog—3 sts.

Bind off with a double decrease bind-off: sl 1 knitwise, k2tog, and psso. Cut yarn, leaving a long tail for sewing to the wreath. Weave in the cast-on end, then gather around the edge of the shape with the bound-off end and pull tight to make a ball.

Small Berry (Make 16)

CO 1 st and knit into the front and back of it—2 sts.

Row 1: Pfb, p1—3 sts.

Row 2: Knit.

Row 3: Purl.

Bind off with a double decrease bind-off: sl 1 knitwise, k2tog, and psso. Cut yarn, leaving a long tail for sewing to the wreath. Weave in the cast-on end, then gather around the edge of the shape with the bound-off end and pull tight to make a ball.

Pin the mistletoe leaves to the wreath and use the cast-on end to sew them in place, just along the stem and the very bottom of the leaves. Then add the berries, two to each pair of leaves.

The wreath with mistletoe added

FIR CONES

• •

Fir cones add some texture to the wreath and make a change from knitting leaves. These are a knitted strip, shaped with short rows and then rolled up and sewn to make the cone shape. You can use various shades of brown for your fir cones; I used three shades. For a frosted effect work the picot bind-off row with cream yarn.

YARN

Approx. 1.4 oz./40 g total for 12 cones.
Sirdar Country Style DK, light weight #3 yarn (40% nylon, 30% wool, 30% acrylic; 170 yd./155 m per 1.7 oz./50 g skein)
• #0530
Stylecraft Special DK, light weight #3 yarn (100% acrylic; 322 yd./295 m per 3.5 oz./100 g skein)
• Walnut
Rowan Pure Wool 4 Ply, light weight #3 yarn (100% wool; 174 yd./160 m per 1.7 oz./50 g skein)
• #461

NEEDLES AND OTHER MATERIALS

• US 3 (3.25 mm) needles
• Tapestry needle

MEASUREMENTS

Big cone: 1.5"/4 cm long
Small cone: 1"/3 cm long

GAUGE

Gauge is not critical.

SPECIAL TECHNIQUES

Cable Cast-On
Make a slip knot and place it on the left-hand needle. Knit a stitch but do not pull it off the left-hand needle; instead transfer the new stitch from right to left needle, leaving two stitches on the left-hand needle. *Now insert the needle between the two stitches, wrap the yarn around the needle as if to knit, and pull the yarn through. Transfer the newly created stitch onto the left-hand needle. Repeat from * until you have the number of stitches needed.
Picot Bind-Off
*CO 2 sts (cable method), BO 3, CO 2, BO 4, rep from * to end of row.

Small and big fir cones

Big Cone (Make 6)

Using the cable method, CO 48 sts.
Row 1: K8, turn (there is no need to wrap the yarn).
Row 2 (and all even-numbered rows): Purl.
Row 3: K16, turn.
Row 5: K24, turn.
Row 7: K32, turn.
Row 9: K40, turn.
Row 11: Knit all 48 sts.
Now, using a lighter shade if you wish, bind off with the picot bind-off. This is the most tedious part of the pattern but it makes all the difference. *CO 2 sts (cable method), BO 3, CO 2, BO 4, rep from * to end of row.
Weave in all the ends and attach a new length of yarn to the cast-on edge at the widest part of the strip. Now roll the strip tightly, with the knit side of the stockinette stitch on the outside. Keep the cast-on edge level so that the other edge spirals. Oversew the edge as you go to hold it all together. When it is all rolled up you will have a long, pointed cone. You can leave it like this or take the yarn up

through the center and back down again to pull it into a squatter shape as I have done. Leave the tail of yarn to sew the cone to the wreath.

Small Cone (Make 6)

Using the cable method, CO 40 sts.
Row 1: K8, turn.
Row 2 (and all even numbered rows): Purl.
Row 3: K16, turn.
Row 5: K24, turn.
Row 7: K32, turn.
Row 9: Knit all 40 sts.

Using a lighter shade if desired, bind off using the picot bind-off, as follows. *CO 2 sts (cable method), BO 3, CO 2, BO 4, rep from * to end of row.

Sew the small cone together in the same way as the big cone.

Pin the fir cones to the wreath (you'll need long pins for this) and then sew them in place using the yarn tails.

Pin and sew the fir cones in place with the yarn tails.

TOADSTOOLS

These toadstools really brighten up the wreath after all that green and brown. They are quite simple to knit. The instructions are for the small toadstool, with variations for the bigger size given in parentheses. I made six large toadstools for the larger wreath, and four small ones for the smaller size.

YARN

Stylecraft Special DK, light weight #3 yarn (100% acrylic; 322 yd./295 m per 3.5 oz./100 g skein)
- 1 skein Lipstick (Color A)
- 1 skein Cream (Color B)

NEEDLES AND OTHER MATERIALS

- US 3 (3.25 mm) needles
- Tapestry needle
- Small amount of stuffing material

MEASUREMENTS

Small toadstool: 1"/3 cm tall
Big toadstool: 1.75"/4.5 cm tall

GAUGE

Gauge is not critical.

STITCH GUIDE

Make 1 (M1)
Make 1 by lifting the thread before the next stitch and knitting into the back of it.

SPECIAL TECHNIQUES

Cable Cast-On
Make a slip knot and place it on the left-hand needle. Knit a stitch but do not pull it off the left-hand needle; instead transfer the new stitch from right to left needle, leaving two stitches on the left-hand needle. *Now insert the needle between the two stitches, wrap the yarn around the needle as if to knit, and pull the yarn through. Transfer the newly created stitch onto the left-hand needle. Repeat from * until you have the number of stitches needed.

Top

Using Color A and the long-tail method, CO 5 sts.
Row 1: Purl.

Sew the toadstools to the wreath; you should only need to attach them at their stalks.

Row 2: K1, M1, k to last st, M1, k1.
Rep these 2 rows until you have 15 (19) sts on your needle.
Next row: Purl.
Next row: Knit.
Next row: Purl.
Next row: Ssk, k to last 2 sts, k2tog.
Rep these last 2 rows until you are back to 7 sts.
Next row: Purl.
BO, leaving a long tail.
Work running stitches just inside the edge of the shape and pull to gather, inserting a small piece of stuffing. Aim for a flat dome rather than a ball. Tidy up the shape by gathering the edge again and then fasten off.

Stalk

Using Color B and the cable cast-on, CO 10 (15) sts.
Work 4 (6) rows in St st.
BO, leaving a long tail.
Roll the stalk sideways, oversewing the cast-on edge as you go, and then sew the side down, too.
Sew the stalk to the top of the toadstool and then add the spots with two or three small stitches here and there.
Pin the toadstools in place and then sew down with Color B yarn. You should only need to sew the stalks down.

HEDGEHOGS

These little hedgehogs are knitted flat and then seamed. You will need two shades of brown yarn.

Big and small hedgehogs

YARN

Lighter color: Stylecraft Special DK, light weight #3 yarn
(100% acrylic; 322 yd./295 m per 3.5 oz./100 g skein)
• 1 skein Mocha
Darker color: Stylecraft Special DK, light weight #3 yarn
(100% acrylic; 322 yd./295 m per 3.5 oz./100 g skein)
• 1 skein Walnut
or
Sirdar Country Style DK, light weight #3 yarn (40% nylon,
30% wool, 30% acrylic; 170 yd./155 m per 1.7 oz./50 g
skein)
• 1 skein #0530

NEEDLES AND OTHER MATERIALS

• US 3 (3.25 mm) needles
• Tapestry needle
• Small amount of stuffing material

MEASUREMENTS

Big hedgehog: 2"/5 cm long
Small hedgehog: 1.5"/4 cm long

GAUGE

Gauge is not critical.

STITCH GUIDE

Make 1 (M1)
Make 1 by lifting the thread before the next stitch and
knitting into the back of it.

Big Hedgehog (Make 4)

Using the lighter color and the long-tail method, CO 3 sts.
Row 1: Purl.
Row 2: K1, M1, k1, M1, k1—5 sts.
Row 3: Purl.
Row 4: K2, M1, k1, M1, k2—7 sts.
Row 5: Purl.
Row 6: K2, M1, k3, M1, k2—9 sts.

Row 7: Purl.
Change to the darker shade.
Row 8: K3, M1, k3, M1, k3—11 sts.
Knit 9 rows without shaping. There will be five dark ridges.
Row 18: Ssk, k7, k2tog—9 sts.
Row 19: Knit.
Row 20: Ssk twice, k1, k2tog twice—5 sts.
Row 21: Knit.
Row 22: Knit.
Row 23: Purl.
Row 24: K1, M1, k3, M1, k1—7 sts.
Row 25: Purl.
Row 26: K1, M1, k5, M1, k1—9 sts.
Row 27: Purl.
Row 28: K1, M1, k7, M1, k1—11 sts.
Work 5 rows in St st beginning with a purl row.
Change back to the lighter shade.
Row 34: Ssk, k7, k2tog—9 sts.
Row 35: Purl.
Row 36: Ssk, k5, k2tog—7 sts.
Row 37: Purl.
Row 38: Ssk, k3, k2tog—5 sts.
Row 39: Ssk, k1, k2tog—3 sts.
BO purlwise.
Oversew the sides together using the tails of yarn; stuff
firmly before closing the last seam.
Add the nose with a few small stitches in the darker yarn.
The eyes are also made with the darker yarn. Take a short
length of yarn and make two knots in the middle of it, one
on top of the other. Then thread each end through from
the eye position (one strand of yarn apart) and come out
in the same place on the bottom of the hedgehog. Knot
the two ends together tightly and weave them in. This will
pull the eyes in a bit and shape the face.

Small Hedgehog (Make 4)

Using the lighter shade and the long-tail method, CO 3 sts.
Row 1: Purl.
Row 2: K1, M1, k1, M1, k1—5 sts.
Row 3: Purl.
Row 4: K2, M1, k1, M1, k2—7 sts.
Row 5: Purl.
Change to the darker shade.
Row 6: K2, M1, k3, M1, k2—9 sts.
Knit 7 rows without shaping. There will be 4 dark ridges.
Row 14: Ssk, k5, k2tog—7 sts.
Row 15: Knit.
Row 16: Ssk, k3, k2tog—5 sts.
Row 17: Knit.
Row 18: Knit.
Row 19: Purl.

Row 20: K1, M1, k3, M1, k1—7 sts.
Row 21: Purl.
Row 22: K1, M1, k5, M1, K1—9 sts.
Row 23: Purl.
Row 24: Knit.
Row 25: Purl.
Change back to the lighter shade.
Row 26: Ssk, k5, k2tog—7 sts.
Row 27: Purl.
Row 28: Ssk, k3, k2tog—5 sts.
Row 29: Ssk, k1, k2tog—3 sts.
BO purlwise.
Finish in the same way as the Big Hedgehog.
Pin the hedgehogs to the wreath and then sew them down using the darker color yarn.

Nestle the hedgehogs in the wreath and sew them down with the darker color yarn.

OWLS

• •

The wreath is getting nicely full now but there's still room for a few owls. The bodies of these are knitted flat and then sewn together, then the wings are knitted and sewn on. The eyes and beak are made out of small scraps of felt.

The owls are knitted in two shades of brown yarn. I've listed the three shades that I mixed and matched for my owls. The instructions are for the small owls, with variations for the bigger ones in parentheses.

YARN

Stylecraft Special DK, light weight #3 yarn (100% acrylic; 322 yd./295 m per 3.5 oz./100 g skein)
• 1 skein Walnut
• 1 skein Mocha
Sirdar Country Style DK, light weight #3 yarn (40% nylon, 30% wool, 30% acrylic; 170 yd./155 m per 1.7 oz./50 g skein)
• 1 skein #0398

NEEDLES AND OTHER MATERIALS

• US 3 (3.25 mm) needles
• Tapestry needle
• Small pieces of light brown and dark brown felt
• Sewing needle and dark brown thread
• Small amount of stuffing material

MEASUREMENTS

Big owl: 1.5"/4 cm tall
Small owl: 1"/3 cm tall

GAUGE

Gauge is not critical.

STITCH GUIDE

Make 1 (M1)
Make 1 by lifting the thread before the next stitch and knitting into the back of it.

Owls in big and small

Body

Using the long-tail method, CO 5 (7) sts.
Row 1: Purl.
Row 2: K1, M1, k to last st, M1, k1—7 (9) sts.
Beginning with a purl row, work 7 (11) rows in St st.
Now make the ears, with the following 6-row pattern.
Row 1: K2, turn.
Row 2: P2.
Row 3: K7 (9).
Row 4: P2, turn.
Row 5: K2.
Row 6: P7 (9).
Now work 6 (10) more rows in St st.
Next row: Ssk, k to last 2 sts, k2tog—5 (7) sts.
BO purlwise.
Fold the body in half and sew the seams, stuffing lightly.

Left Wing

Using the long-tail method, CO 3 sts.
Row 1: Purl.
Row 2: K1, M1, k2—4 sts.
Row 3: Purl.
Row 4: K1, M1, k3—5 sts.
Row 5: Purl.
Bigger size only:
Row 6: K1, M1, k4—6 sts.
Row 7: Purl.
Row 8: K4, k2tog—5 sts.
Row 9: Purl.
Both sizes:
Next row: K3, k2tog—4 sts.
Next row: Purl.
BO, knitting the last 2 sts together.
Sew to the owl's body with the bound-off edge at the top.

Right Wing

This is a reversed version of the Left Wing.
Using the long-tail method, CO 3 sts.
Row 1: Purl.
Row 2: K2, M1, k1—4 sts.
Row 3: Purl.

Row 4: K3, M1, k1—5 sts.
Row 5: Purl.
Bigger size only:
Row 6: K4, M1, k1—6 sts.
Row 7: Purl.
Row 8: Ssk, k4—5 sts.
Row 9: Purl.
Both sizes:
Next row: Ssk, k3—4 sts.
Next row: Purl.
BO, working ssk on the first 2 sts.
Sew to the owl's body.

Eyes and Beak

Cut two small circles in felt for each eye, one smaller than the other. I cut mine freehand, holding the scissors still and moving the felt. Sew the eyes to the face with small stitches using light yarn or thread.

The beak is a long triangle with the top corners trimmed off. Sew it to the owl's face with sewing thread, just along the top. If you catch the bottom of the beak down with a few stitches positioned slightly higher than the bottom of the felt, the beak will curve outward.

Pin the owls to the wreath and sew in place using the lighter color of yarn.

Small and large wreaths with owls in place

FAT FLOWERS

These flowers are knitted flat and only need a little sewing up to transform them into puffy flowers. As well as adding color to the Woodland Wreath, they could be used to decorate lots of other things. They can be knitted in any yarn, but work to a fairly firm tension for the best finished shape.

YARN

Sirdar Country Style DK, light weight #3 yarn (40% nylon, 30% wool, 30% acrylic; 170 yd./155 m per 1.7 oz./50 g skein)
- 1 skein #0418 red
- 1 skein #0527 pink
- Small amount of contrasting color for centers

NEEDLES AND OTHER MATERIALS

- US 3 (3.25 mm) needles
- Tapestry needle

MEASUREMENTS

Big fat flower: 2"/5 cm
Small fat flower: 1.5"/4 cm

GAUGE

Gauge is not critical.

STITCH GUIDE

Slip 1 (sl 1)
In this pattern, slip stitches purlwise with the yarn in front.
Slip 2, Knit, Pass Slipped Stitches Over (S2KP2)
Slip 2 sts as if to knit them together, knit 1 st, and pass slipped stitches over—2 sts decreased.

SPECIAL TECHNIQUES

Cable Cast-On
Make a slip knot and place it on the left-hand needle. Knit a stitch but do not pull it off the left-hand needle; instead transfer the new stitch from right to left needle, leaving two stitches on the left-hand needle. *Now insert the needle between the two stitches, wrap the yarn around the needle as if to knit, and pull the yarn through. Transfer the newly created stitch onto the left-hand needle. Repeat from * until you have the number of stitches needed.

Completed big and small fat flowers in red and pink

Big Flower

Using the cable cast-on, CO 6 sts.
Row 1: [Kfb] 6 times—12 sts.
Row 2 and all even-numbered rows: Purl.
Row 3: [K1, kfb] 6 times—18 sts.
Row 5: [K2, kfb] 6 times—24 sts.
Row 7: [K3, kfb] 6 times—30 sts.
Row 8: Purl.
That's one side of the flower done. The next 2 rows make the eyelets around the edge, which shape the petals.
Row 9: [K3, yo, k2tog] 6 times.
Row 10: Purl.
Now decrease for the second side of the flower.
Row 11: [K3, k2tog] 6 times—24 sts.
Row 12 and all even-numbered rows: Purl.
Row 13: [K2, k2tog] 6 times—18 sts.
Row 15: [K1, k2tog] 6 times—12 sts.
Row 17: [K2tog] 6 times—6 sts.
Now, with the purl side facing you, BO purlwise, leaving a long tail.
Sew up the side seam, giving you a lantern shape. Resist the temptation to close the holes at the top and bottom; you're going to need them. Now flatten your shape out so that the two holes are on top of each other and pull your needle up through both holes.

Around the edge of your circle will be the six eyelets; these mark the lines between the petals. Take your needle over the edge at one of these eyelets and back up through the center holes. Pull the yarn tight to pull the edge of the petal in and then go over the next eyelet. Continue like this all around the circle until you have marked all six petals. Remember to pull the yarn tight each time. When you have gone all the way around, make a small stitch to hold the tension. If you are going to add a button to the center, you can do this now.

To add an embroidered center, fasten off your yarn and find a long length of a contrasting color. To embroider the flower center, bring your yarn about halfway up the line between two petals and then down through the center, making a straight stitch. Do the same thing to make a stitch opposite the first one, and then work around the flower making two more pairs of stitches in the same way. Now repeat this for six more lines, this time making them longer and positioning them in the center of the petals.

The eyelets around the edge of your circle mark the petals. Take your needle over the edge at one of these eyelets and back up through the center hole. Pull the yarn tight to pull in the edge of the petal, and then go to the next eyelet, doing the same thing, and then repeating all around the circle.

After Row 17, once you sew up the side seam, your knitting will be in a lantern shape.

Embroider the flower center with straight stitches between the petals.

Small Flower

These are worked in the same way as the big flowers but you stop increasing at 24 sts rather than 30.

Using the cable cast-on, CO 6 sts.

Row 1: [Kfb] 6 times—12 sts.
Row 2 and all even-numbered rows: Purl.
Row 3: [K1, kfb] 6 times—18 sts.
Row 5: [K2, kfb] 6 times—24 sts.
Row 7: [K2, yo, k2tog] 6 times.
Row 9: [K2, k2tog] 6 times—18 sts.
Row 11: [K1, k2tog] 6 times—12 sts.
Row 13: [K2tog] 6 times—6 sts.

BO purlwise and finish in the same way as for the big flower.

Flatten the knitting so that the two holes are on top of each other and pull your needle up through both holes.

BLUEBELLS

The last things to add to the wreath are some bluebells. You would normally see masses of bluebells together in a wood, but I have added just six stems to each of my wreaths. Each stem has two bluebell flowers and, again, they come in two sizes.

YARN

Bluebells: Stylecraft Special DK, light weight #3 yarn (100% acrylic; 322 yd./295 m per 3.5 oz./100 g skein)
- 1 skein Bluebell

Stems: Sirdar Snuggly DK, light weight #3 yarn (55% nylon, 45% acrylic; 179 yd./165 m per 1.7 oz./50 g skein)
- 1 skein #0442

NEEDLES AND OTHER MATERIALS

- US 3 (3.25 mm) needles
- US 5 (3.75 mm) double-pointed needles
- Tapestry needle

MEASUREMENTS

Big bluebells: 1"/3 cm long with 4"/10 cm stem
Small bluebells: .75"/2 cm long with 3"/8 cm stem

GAUGE

Gauge is not critical.

STITCH GUIDE

Make 1 (M1)
Make 1 by lifting the thread before the next stitch and knitting into the back of it.

SPECIAL TECHNIQUES

I-Cord
Knit every row but don't turn the work at the ends of the rows. Slide the stitches to the other end of the needle, pull the yarn around from behind the stitches, and knit again.

Big Bluebell (Make 12)

Using the long-tail method and size 3 (3.25 mm) needles, CO 6 sts.
Row 1: Purl.
Row 2: K1, [M1, k2] twice, M1, k1—9 sts.
Beginning with a purl row, work 5 rows in St st.

Big and small bluebells on stems

Next row: [Kfb] 9 times—18 sts.
BO knitwise, leaving a long tail.
Darn in the cast-on tail. Using the bind-off tail, join the side seam and gather the cast-on edge. Leave the tail for sewing the flower to the stem.

Small Bluebell (Make 12)

Using the long-tail method and size 3 (3.25 mm) needles, CO 4 sts.
Row 1: Purl.
Row 2: K1, [M1, k1] 3 times—7 sts.
Beginning with a purl row, work 3 rows in St st.
Next row: [Kfb] 7 times—14 sts.
BO knitwise and finish in the same way as the Big Bluebells.

Stems

Using the long-tail method and size 5 (3.75 mm) double-pointed needles, CO 3 sts.
Work 30 rows in I-cord for the bigger bluebells and 20 for the smaller. The stems should measure either 4"/10 cm or 3"/8 cm.

BO with the double decrease bind-off: slip one stitch knitwise, k2tog, and pass the slipped stitch over.

Weave in the ends.

Sew one bluebell to the side of the top of the stem with a small vertical stitch. Leave a small amount of yarn between the flower and the stem so that it hangs nicely. Now sew another bluebell a little below the top of the stem.

Pin the bluebells in place on the wreath and sew down along the stem.

Bluebells sewn to wreath

Fat flower sewn to wreath

Holiday Cables Hat

E very winter outfit should have a pop of color, and this hat looks great knitted in any color. Give it as a gift in the favorite color of the recipient or knit it for yourself in red to show your Christmas spirit. Set it at a jaunty angle and head out for some holiday shopping.

YARN

Lion Brand Vanna's Choice, medium weight #4 yarn (100% premium acrylic; 170 yd./156 m per 3.5 oz./100 g skein
• 1 skein Cranberry

NEEDLES AND OTHER MATERIALS

• 1 set US 9 (5.5 mm) double-pointed needles
• Cable needle
• Stitch marker
• Tapestry needle

MEASUREMENTS

Circumference: 23.5"/60 cm

GAUGE

18 sts x 24 rows in cable patt = 4"/10 cm square
Adjust needle size if necessary to obtain gauge.

STITCH GUIDE

C10B
Slip next 5 sts to cable needle and hold to the back of work, knit 5 sts from left needle, knit 5 sts from cable needle.
Make 1 (M1)
Make 1 by lifting the thread before the next stitch and knitting into the back of it.

Hat

CO 90 sts (30 sts on each of 3 needles). Join to knit in the round, being careful not to twist the sts; pm for end of round.
Rnds 1–6: Knit.
Rnd 7: Purl.
Rnds 8–13: Knit.
Rnd 14: Purl.
Rnd 15: *[K3, M1] 4 times, k3; rep from * around—114 sts.

Cable Pattern

Rnd 1: K1, *p1, k5, p1, k12; rep from * around, ending last repeat k11.
Rnd 2: *P1, k1, p1, k3, p1, k1, p1, C10B; rep from * around.
Rnd 3: K1, *p1, k5, p1, k12; rep from * around, ending last repeat k11.
Rnd 4: *P1, k1, p1, k3, p1, k1, p1, k10; rep from * around.
Rnds 5–12: Rep Rnds 3–4 of cable pattern (4 times each).

Rnd 13: K1, *p1, k5, p1, k12; rep from * around, ending last repeat k11.
Rnd 14: *P1, k1, p1, k3, p1, k1, p1, C10B; rep from * around.
Rnds 15–26: Rep Rnds 3–14.
Rnd 27: K1, *p1, k5, p1, k12; rep from * around, ending last repeat k11.
Rnd 28: *P1, k1, p1, k3, p1, k1, p1, k10; rep from * around.

Crown Shaping

Rnd 1: *K1, k2tog; rep from * around—76 sts.
Rnd 2: Knit.
Rnd 3: K2tog around—38 sts.
Rnd 4: Knit.
Rnd 5: K2tog around—19 sts.
Break yarn leaving a 12"/30.5 cm end. Draw through 19 sts tightly and fasten securely.

Finishing

Fold under facing at turning ridge and hem to wrong side. Steam block.

Holly Hat

This super-cute hat is not just for the kiddies. It comes in sizes from Newborn to Adult. A pretty picot edging and holly leaves and berries give this hat its vintage chic look. Given as a gift, it will really show the time and detail that you put into it.

Shown in Child size.

YARN

Light weight #3 yarn, 3.5 oz./100 g
• 1 ball cream
Super fine #1 yarn, 1.7 oz./50 g
• 1 ball green
• 1 ball red

NEEDLES AND OTHER MATERIALS

• US 6 (4 mm) 12"/30 cm or 16"/40 cm long circular needle
• US 6 (4 mm) set of double-pointed needles
• US 2 (2.75 mm) straight needles
• US E-4 (3.5 mm) crochet hook
• Stitch markers
• Tapestry needle
• Scissors

SIZES/MEASUREMENTS

Newborn (3–6 Months, 6–12 Months, Toddler, Child, Adult)
Unstretched circumference: 11 (13, 14.5, 16, 17.5, 19)"/28 (33, 37, 41, 45, 48) cm
Note: To determine which size to make, measure head circumference just above the ears and subtract 2–3"/5–7.5 cm. The hat will stretch a few inches once completed.

GAUGE

20 sts x 28 rows on size 6 (4 mm) needles = 4"/10 cm square
Adjust needle sizes if necessary to obtain gauge. Gauge is extremely important on hats to ensure proper fit.

STITCH GUIDE

Kfbf
Knit in front, back, and front again of the same stitch—2 stitches increased.

Hat

With cream yarn and circular needle, CO 56 (64, 72, 80, 88, 96) sts. Place a stitch marker to mark beginning of round. Join to work in the round, being careful not to twist work.
Rnds 1–2: [K2, p2] rep to end of rnd.
Rnd 3: [(K2tog but leave both sts on left needle, insert right needle into the top st and knit it again, then slide both sts off the left needle), p2] rep to end of rnd.
Rnds 4–6: [K2, p2] rep to end of rnd.
Rnd 7: Rep Rnd 3.
Rnd 8: [K2, p2] rep to end of rnd.

Rnds 9–20: Knit.
Rnd 21: K2, [p1, k7] rep to last 6 sts, p1, k5.
Rnd 22: K1, [p1, k1, p1, k5] rep to last 7 sts, p1, k1, p1, k4.
Rnd 23: K2, [p1, k7] rep to last 6 sts, p1, k5.
Rnds 24–25: Knit.
Rnd 26: K6, [p1, k7] rep to last 2 sts, p1, k1.
Rnd 27: [K5, p1, k1, p1] rep to end of rnd.
Rnd 28: K6, [p1, k7] rep to last 2 sts, p1, k1.
Rnds 29–30: Knit.
Rep Rnds 21–30 until piece measures 4 (4.5, 5, 5.5, 6, 6.25)"/10 (11.5, 13, 14, 15, 16) cm from beginning.

Shape Top

Rnd 1: [K6, k2tog] rep to end of rnd—49 (56, 63, 70, 77, 84) sts.
Rnd 2: Knit.
Rnd 3: [K5, k2tog] rep to end of rnd—42 (48, 54, 60, 66, 72) sts.
Rnd 4: Knit.
Rnd 5: [K4, k2tog] rep to end of rnd—35 (40, 45, 50, 55, 60) sts.
Rnd 6: Switch to dpns and knit.
Rnd 7: [K3, k2tog] rep to end of rnd—28 (32, 36, 40, 44, 48) sts.
Rnd 8: Knit.
Rnd 9: [K2, k2tog] rep to end of rnd—21 (24, 27, 30, 33, 36) sts.
Rnd 10: Knit.
Rnd 11: [K1, k2tog] rep to end of rnd—14 (16, 18, 20, 22, 24) sts.
Rnd 12: [K2tog] rep to end of rnd—7 (8, 9, 10, 11, 12) sts.
Rnd 13: [K2tog] rep to end of rnd—4 (4, 5, 5, 6, 6) sts.
Sizes 6–12 Month, Toddler, Child, Adult: Rep Rnd 13 until 4 sts remain.
All sizes: Place remaining 4 sts onto one dpn and work a 4-stitch I-cord for .75–1"/1.9–2.5 cm. Bind off. Cut yarn. Weave in ends on wrong side of hat.

Picot Edge

Using cream yarn and crochet hook, pull a loop up through a stitch along the cast-on row (bottom) of hat. Chain 3, slip stitch in same stitch. [Single crochet in next stitch, (slip stitch, chain 3, slip stitch) in next stitch] repeat to end of round. Slip stitch into base of beginning chain 3. Cut yarn. Weave in ends on wrong side of hat.

Holly (Make 10)

With green yarn and size US 2 (2.75 mm) needles, CO 18 sts.
Row 1: Knit.
Row 2: Purl.
Row 3: Knit.
Row 4: K1, [yo, k2tog] rep to last st, k1.
Row 5: Knit.
Row 6: Purl.
Row 7: Knit.
Row 8: Bind off knitwise.
Fold leaf in half lengthwise and stitch the cast-on and bind-off edges together.
Fold leaf in half end to end and stitch up the center with the bumps on the outside edge to form the leaf.
Sew finished leaves onto hat around lower band in groups of two.

Berries (Make 15)

With red yarn and size US 2 (2.75 mm) needles, CO 1 st.
Row 1: Kfbf—3 sts.
Row 2: Knit.
Row 3: Purl.
Row 4: Knit, pass first 2 sts over last. Cut yarn and pull end through.
Gather tightly into a ball. Sew onto hat in groups of three in center of two-leaf groupings.

Design by Jennifer Wilby/Ladyship Designs

Poinsettia Pillow

Inspired by the cheerful plant that brings a splash of color during the winter months, I designed this poinsettia pillow cover. It has a three-button envelope closure, which makes it easy to remove when you want to wash it or change your seasonal décor. The main part of the pillow is knitted in stockinette stitch as one piece. The leaves and petals are knit separately and sewn into place.

YARN

Medium weight #4 yarn
- 7 oz./200 g white
- 3.5 oz./100 g red
- 1.7 oz./50 g green
- Small amount yellow

NEEDLES AND OTHER MATERIALS

- US 6 (4 mm) knitting needles
- US 8 (5 mm) knitting needles
- Tapestry needle

MEASUREMENTS

16 x 16"/40 x 40 cm

GAUGE

16 sts x 24 rows in St st with US 8 (5 mm) needles = 4"/10 cm square

Adjust needle size if necessary to obtain gauge.

Pillow Cover

Using white yarn and US 6 (4 mm) needles, CO 65 sts.
Work in K1, P1 Rib as follows:

Row 1: *K1, p1; rep from * to last st, k1.

Row 2: *P1, k1; rep from * to last st, p1.

Rep Rows 1–2 until 6 rows have been worked.

Make Buttonholes

Row 7: Work Rib for 16 sts, BO 3 sts, work Rib for 12 sts, BO 3 sts, work Rib for 12 sts, BO 3 sts, work Rib for 16 sts.

Row 8: Work Rib for 16 sts, CO 3 sts, work Rib for 12 sts, CO 3 sts, work Rib for 12 sts, CO 3 sts, work Rib for 16 sts.

Rows 9–14: Continue in Rib pattern as set.

Change to US 8 (5 mm) needles and work in stockinette stitch (knit one row, purl one row) until work measures 32"/81 cm from cast-on edge. At this point, stretch your work around your chosen pillow form. The working edge should meet with the cast-on edge with a little stretch. A well-stuffed pillow may need a few more rows of knitting.

Change to US 6 (4 mm) needles and work K1, P1 Rib as follows:

Row 1: *K1, p1; rep from * to last st, k1.

Row 2: *P1, k1; rep from * to last st, p1.

Rep Rows 1–2 until 14 rows have been completed.

Poinsettia

Green Leaves (Make 3)

Using green yarn and US 8 (5 mm) needles, CO 5 sts.
Row 1: K1, kfb, k1, kfb, k1—7 sts.
Row 2 and all even rows: Purl.
Row 3: K2, kfb, k1, kfb, k2—9 sts.
Row 5: K3, kfb, k1, kfb, k3—11 sts.
Row 7: K4, kfb, k1, kfb, k4—13 sts.
Row 9: K5, kfb, k1, kfb, k5—15 sts.
Rows 11 and 13: Ssk, k4, kfb, k1, kfb, k4, k2tog—15 sts.
Row 15: Ssk, k11, k2tog—13 sts.
Row 17: Ssk, k9, k2tog—11 sts.
Row 19: Ssk, k7, k2tog—9 sts.
Row 21: Ssk, k5, k2tog—7 sts.
Row 23: Ssk, k3, k2tog—5 sts.
Row 25: Ssk, k1, k2tog—3 sts.
Row 27: Sl 1, k2tog, psso. Fasten off.

Red Petals (Make 12)

Using red yarn and US 8 (5 mm) needles, CO 5 sts.
Row 1: K1, kfb, k1, kfb, k1—7 sts.
Row 2 and all even rows: Purl.
Row 3: K2, kfb, k1, kfb, k2—9 sts.
Row 5: K3, kfb, k1, kfb, k3—11 sts.
Row 7: K4, kfb, k1, kfb, k4—13 sts.
Rows 9 and 11: Ssk, k3, kfb, k1, kfb, k3, k2tog—13 sts.
Row 13: Ssk, k9, k2tog—11 sts.
Row 15: Ssk, k7, k2tog—9 sts.
Row 17: Ssk, k5, k2tog—7 sts.
Row 19: Ssk, k3, k2tog—5 sts.
Row 21: Ssk, k1, k2tog—3 sts.
Row 23: Sl 1, k2tog, psso. Fasten off.

Yellow Bobbles (Make 3)

Using yellow yarn and US 8 (5 mm) needles, CO 1 st and make into 5 sts by knitting into the front and back of same st three times.
Row 1: Purl.
Row 2: Knit.
Row 3: Purl.
Row 4: Knit.
Row 5: With RH needle, pull second, third, fourth, and fifth sts over first st and off the LH needle one by one. Fasten off last remaining st.

Finishing

Weave in any loose ends. Block.

Find and mark the center of the front square of the pillow. Sew on green leaves around this center mark. Add red leaves one layer at a time. Finally, add yellow bobbles to center of flower, pulling into spherical shape as you stitch them in place.

With wrong side facing and ribbing overlapped, sew up both side seams using your preferred method, making sure that the flower is in the center front of the pillow. Turn work right side out, sew on buttons to match buttonholes, add pillow insert, and enjoy!

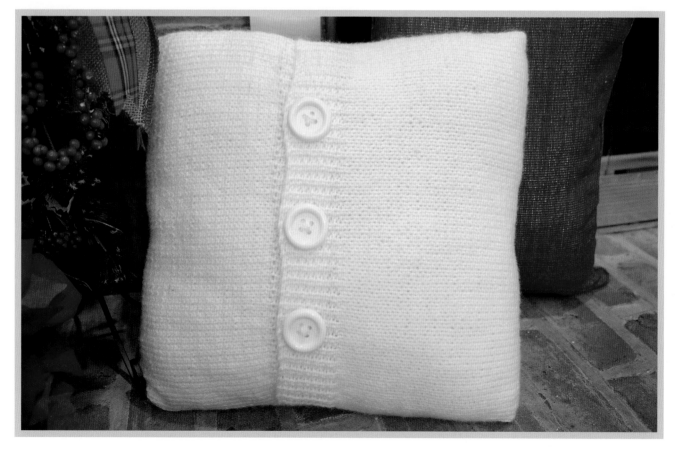

Abbreviations

BO	bind off
CC	contrasting color
CO	cast on
dec	decrease
k	knit
k2tog	knit 2 together
kfb	knit in front and back
kfbf	knit in front and back and front
inc	increase
M1	make 1
MC	main color
p	purl
p2tog	purl 2 together
pfb	purl in front and back
pm	place marker
psso	pass slipped stitch over
PU	pick up and knit
rep	repeat
rnd	round
S2KP2	slip 2, knit, pass slipped stitches over
sl	slip
ssk	slip, slip, knit
sm	slip marker
St st	stockinette stitch

Contributors

Martha Johnson/Fiddlestyx
Fiddlestyx.com
fiddlestyx@live.com

Frankie Brown/Frankie's Knitted Stuff
http://www.ravelry.com/patterns/sources/frankies-knitted-stuff

Jennifer Wilby/Ladyship Designs
LadyshipDesigns.etsy.com
LadyshipDesigns@gmail.com

Vicky Gordon/Knitting By Post
KnittingByPost.co.uk

Sara Elizabeth Kellner/Rabbit Hole Knits
RabbitHoleKnits.com

Alma Mahler/Heaven to Seven
https://www.etsy.com/shop/heaventoseven

Amy Munson
http://www.ravelry.com/patterns/sources/amy-munson-designs
https://www.etsy.com/shop/amymunsondesigns

Thank you to our stocking sample knitters:
Christen Comer
Candice Derr
Anna Fulton
Kathryn Fulton

Visual Index

Kris Kringle's Christmas Tree 2

Santa Jack 7

Down the Chimney 11

Reindeer Games 15

Paper Dolls 20

Norwegian Flowers 23

Pretty Plaid 26

Jolly Old St. Nick 29

Night Sleigh 34

With Bells On 39

Snowman 44

Candy Cane Christmas 49

Scandinavian Star Slippers 54

Children's Scandinavian Slippers 58

Santa Pajama Case 62

Colorwork Ornaments 66

Stormy Dawn Hobby Horse 79

Santa Booties 83

Woodland Wreath 85

Holiday Cables Hat 111

Holly Hat 113

Poinsettia Pillow 116